Rūmī and the Whirling Dervishes

Alberto Fabio Ambrosio

Rūmī and the Whirling Dervishes

Alberto Fabio Ambrosio

ATF Theology
Adelaide
2019

A Forum for Theology in the World
Volume 6, Issue 2, 2019

A Forum for Theology in the World is an academic refereed journal aimed at engaging with issues in the contemporary world, a world which is pluralist and ecumenical in nature. The journal reflects this pluralism and ecumenism. Each edition is theme specific and has its own editor responsible for the production. The journal aims to elicit and encourage dialogue on topics and issues in contemporary society and within a variety of religious traditions. The Editor in Chief welcomes submissions of manuscripts, collections of articles, for review from individuals or institutions, which may be from seminars or conferences or written specifically for the journal. An internal peer review is expected before submitting the manuscript. It is the expectation of the publisher that, once a manuscript has been accepted for publication, it will be submitted according to the house style to be found at the back of this volume. All submissions to the Editor in Chief are to be sent to: hdregan@atf.org.au.

Each edition is available as a journal subscription, or as a book in print, pdf or epub, through the ATF Press web site — www.atfpress.com. Journal subscriptions are also available through EBSCO and other library suppliers.

Editor in Chief
Hilary Regan, ATF Press

A Forum for Theology in the World is published by ATF Theology and imprint of ATF (Australia) Ltd (ABN 90 116 359 963) and is published twice or three times a year.

ISBN: 978-1-925612-25-7 soft
978-1-925612-26-4 hard
978-1-925612-27-1 epub
978-1-925612-28-8 pdf

ATF Press
PO Box 504
Hindmarsh SA 5007
Australia
www.atfpress.com

A Forum for Theology in the World Vol 6 No 2/2019

Table of Contents

Introduction

Sufism has had, at times, a difficult history in Islam and also within Western culture. Since the beginning of the religious tradition begun by the Prophet Muhammad, Sufism has been misunderstood even within Islam itself. It is considered by many that with the martyrdom of al-Hallâj, one of the most important personalities of the history of Sufism, murdered in 922, the separation, or the break, between Sufism and a more orthodox form of Islam started. Since that time, there is an interpretation that has read the history of Sufism as a form of unofficial Islam, or even—and this is much worse—an *heterodox* form of Islam. There is within the history of Islam, many preachers, doctors of law and theologians who have criticised Sufism for a variety reasons. For many, Sufism is an esoteric interpretation of the Qur'an and the message of the Prophet. Thus, estorericism is grounded in the idea that the Prophet Muhammad had transmitted in some occult manner a more profound message to a small number of disciples; the 'chosen' so to speak. Because of the possibility of an esoteric interpretation, Sufism has developed a sense of 'election' and since then, the existence of an 'élite', a level upper level, above the masses, to whom the official message was revealed. Above this élite, there was even an 'élite of the élite', a small number of people who understood things in an even more profound manner.

The existence of an 'élite' who had received a special authority to learn the spiritual interpretation of the Qur'an could not be appreciated by other official theologians, doctors of law or more orthodox interpreters. Sufism is thus at the origin of a spiritual lineage that sometimes can be understood as a parallel way of the religious authority which does not really exist in more mainstream dimensions of Islam. These two points: the existence of a special and a more profound message revealed just to an 'élite', and the spiritual authority of this 'élite', are also accompanied by a special doctrine. Among sections of this doctrine, there is one point which has been raised in the history of Sufism and Islam.

Since al-Hallâj, the most problematic point is the idea that there is no other real existence than of God Himself. The true and real being is just God Himself. The creatures of the God creator are nothing other than some reflections of the divinity. This doctrine is explained in a very extended way by the mystical Philosopher Ibn 'Arabî (d 1240) in his numerous writings. He did not give a real name to this doctrine, but his disciples did: they named it as the unicity of existence (*wahdât al-wujûd*). God is the only one being and the creatures are just manifestations (*tajalliyât*) of the divinity. This doctrine is a further interpretation of the fundamental creed of Islam: there is no divinity other than God (lâ ilâh illâ Allâh). The Sufis went much further asserting that there is no being other than God. Eventually, official Islam could have accepted this element as strange as it might sound, but the consequence of such a doctrine is that the creature is nothing. If the creature is just a manifestion as reflection, or even nothing—because God is the only existing One—then the creature is also God.

One tendency in the Sufi tradition is to think that the only real existing being is God's being. All creatures do not have a status of real being. They are like manifestations, a reflection of God's being. And if creatures are just 'manifestations' of God, without any real metaphysical status, then they are 'nothing'. But if the only One existing is God and the creatures are nothing, it means that they are in someway God's manifestation, a manifestation of God.

For this reason, al-Hallâj affirmed that he was the divine reality (*anâ al-Hâqq*), or translated as 'I am God'. In one understanding, Hallâj was not so much asserting that he was God, he was simply stating that only God exists. The guardians of the orthodox interpretation could not really accept such ideas from Sufism. A number of theologians, for example Muhammad al-Ghazâlî (d 1111), reintegrated Sufism into a wider treaty of Islamic doctrine. From the eleventh century Sufism has been received another attitude by many Islamic scholars. Even with the intervention of a such important and influent theologian as Ghazâlî, Sufism has continued to raise quite a number doubts among scholars and believers. These doubts and suspicions sometimes became a real persecution in order to purify the Islamic creed and thus to allow condemnation by the Islamic world.

The following five chapters are the result of ten years of research on a particular Sufi order (*tarîqa*) or way of spiritual life. The history of Sufism can be described in three important historical steps. First, the period of charismatic figures such an al-Hallâj among many others. They gave the pillars of the future Sufi doctrine, they also gave the fundamental elements of the practices such as the *dhikr*, the repetition of the name of Allâh. These personalities received also some critics and at times an open persecution. Second, from the seventh century to the twelfth century, the time of the birth of Sufism as a doctrine and practices. The third, from the twelfth century on, is the time of the 'instituionalisation' of Sufism by the birth of the Sufi orders.

From the very beginning, there were four fundamental Sufi orders and many new branches and under a rule and constitutions, Sufi orders. A Sufi order is not like a Catholic religious order where religious people live together, but a group of disciples who gather around a founder, or the vicar of the founder, the living master. From the beginning Sufism is founded on a chain (a gold chain, *silsila*) relying on a founder through to the present-day master by a transmission of the spiritual authority (*ijazâ*).

The case that is presented here is that of the famous so called whirling dervishes doctrines and practices, in a very academic way. The Mevlevîyye—the real name of the Sufi order—is inspired and partially founded by Rûmî, and has become very famous in western languages, but there have not been many academic studies on this topic. The eighth anniversary of the birth of the founder, Mevlânâ Jelâl ed-dîn Rûmî (1209–1273), was the occasion for a number of international conferences and studies in Turkey as well as in the rest of the world. Since then academic works have grown, but in western languages they are very few.

The first chapter in this volume is a study on Rûmî, the great mystic poet of Islam who wrote in Persian, and his Son, Sultân Veled. This is a particular and complex history that details the tensions of the history of Mevlevîs: between the veneration of the founder, the charismatic one, and the institutionalisation by the family more oriented in to preserving and conserving the richness of the founder than pursuing the charisma itself. This is obviously the history of many religious movements which brings the difference between the charisma which began movement and the institutionalization over time. Nevertheless, for the whirling dervishes—the poor translation of *mevlevîs*—shows a tension between the charisma and the institution, the love and the discipline, the mysticism and the practice.

The second chapter analyses the most important practice of the all Sufis, the *dhikr*, the repetiton of the name of *Allâh*. The whirling dervishes practiced the *dhikr,* and not just the dance (*semâ'*), the very famous and spectacular codified ritual of a whirling dance. The chapter explains that *dhikr* is primordial in the *mevlevîyye*. That is, without understanding the role of the *dhikr* in *mevlevî* daily life, the *semâ'* is not understandable. The *dhikr* is compared by one of the most significant *mevlevî*, Ismaîl Ankaravî (d 1631) to the castle of God, meaning a religious practice that protects people performing it. This affirmation has also permitted the study to establish some interesting comparisons with Christian mysticism, especially that of Therese of Avila and her 'inner castle'.

The seventeenth Ottoman century is the time of the organisation of a campaign against Sufis and their practices. Sufism was considered so related to the devil that they were held responsible of the military decline of the Ottoman Empire. In my view it is the avant-première of the Wahhabism doctrine's organisation in the eighteenth Arabian peninsula's time. The Ottoman Sultan was so influenced by the movement called the *Qâdîzâdelî* (the sons of the judge), that he was obliged to condemn the *semâ'* practice. It was 1666, and the chronicles say that during this year the ban of the *semâ'* became official, even if after just one year from then that the Sufis, and especially the *Mevlevîs* found the way to again perform their mystical dance.

Mevlevîs have had a fertile history in literary, religious thought and musical production. That is why, we can still find and try to configure a *mevlevî* library. Thanks to the living collection, and to the existing academic writings, it is possible to analyse a 'hypothetical' *mevlevî* library at the end of the Ottoman Empire or at the end of the eighteenth century and beginning of the nineteenth century. The founder of the modern Turkey, Mustafa Kemal Atatürk (d 1938), banned in a General Assembly, (held in 1925,) all the Sufi orders and also confiscated all their buildings and proprieties. Since that time, by painstaking study, it the references whirling dervishes library has been reconstituted, in order to understand the nature and extent of such a 'culture', principally because the *mevlevî* is a culture and not just *semâ'* practice or mystical writings or poems.

The fifth chapter is an inquiry into the profound doctrine of love of Rûmî and his commentator Ismaîl Ankaravî. Rûmî was and is still known as the founder of the Sufi path of love, or even the religion of love. In his many poems, he speaks of the religion of love. Sometimes, in the history of the interpretation of Rûmî's works and thought it has been opposed to Ibn 'Arabî's thought. Rûmî's works are affective and love oriented, while Ibn 'Arabî's are oriented to the oneness and a more intellectual approach. Instead of being in opposition, both are in some way, they are two different languages or thought paths, and not just because Rûmî wrote in Persian and Ibn 'Arabî in Arabic. Rûmî is a great mystic because of his sense of infinite love, that is without any limit as God Himself has no limit. This interpretation of love by Rûmî lets the reader consider effectively Islam as a religion of love and not just of the law. In Sufim there is the possibility to establish a meaning of eternal love and to link it to God. Rûmî is an Islamic scholar, before being a Sufi. He knew very well the classical doctrine and even if he moved on from a classical interpretation, he remained anchored to Muhammad and his message.

The five chapters offer a possibility to know Rûmî and his Sufi order, *Mevlevîyye*, in a more academic way, one which is open to a mystical doctrine. By re-reading elements of the history of the whirling dervishes, especially in the dimension of the mystical practices and their impact, it allows the possibility to consider Islam as an official, classic and orthodox religion and on the other hand as an unofficial, modern and *heterodox* religion.

Along the way, in all of this, the reader can make comparisons with Christian theology, practices and spirituality, and this interface and connection is important for the aim of this journal.

I wish to acknowledge and thank Hilary Regan and ATF Press Publishing Group for making this collection possible and making these papers accessible to a wider English speaking audience in this edition of *A Forum for Theology in the World.*

Alberto F Ambrosio OP
Luxembourg/Paris
November 2019

Acknowledgments

With thanks for the permissions for the following articles and their respective publications in which they were first published. We decided to keep the transcription system for each chapter the one we used for each publication.

Chapter I: '"The Son is the Secret of the Father": Rūmī, Sultān Veled and the Strategy of Family Feelings', in Catherine Mayeur-Jaouen, Alexandre Papas, editors, *Family Portraits with Saints. Hagiography, Sanctity and Family in the Muslim World* (Berlin: Klaus Schwarz Verlag, 2014), 308–326.

Chapter II: 'The Castle of God is the Centre of the Dervish's Soul', in *Mawlana Rumi Review*, 1 (2010): 82–99.

Chapter III: 'İsmā'īl Rusūhī Ankaravī: An Early Mevlevi Intervention into the Emerging Kadızadeli-Sufi Conflict', in J Curry and E Ohlander, editors *Sufism and Society. Arrangements of the Mystical in the Muslim World, 1200-1800*, (London: Routledge, 2011), 182–197.

Chapter IV: 'The Library of the Whirling Dervish: An Editorial Policy', in Rachida Chih, Catherine Mayeur-Jaouen and Rüdiger Seesemann, editors, *Sufism, Literary Production, and Printing in the Nineteenth Century* (Würzburg: Ergon Verlag, 2015), 75–98.

Chapter V: 'Boundless Love: Ismā'īl Anqarawī's Commentary on the Preface to the Second Book of the Mathnawī', in *Mawlana Rumi Review*, 3 (2012): 68–94.

A Forum for Theology in the World Vol 6 No 2/2019

'The Son is the Secret of the Father' Rûmî, Sultân Veled and the Strategy of Family Feelings

The relation between the great Master Rûmî (d 1273),[1] the founder or—in some other worlds—the inspirer of the Mevleviye sufi Order, and his son Sultân Veled (d 1312) is an enormous field for penetrating the family's sainthood. The familiar history of Rûmî could represent to itself a vast topic for more than a paper, probably a deep study. Regarding to the posterity of Rûmî, the family's relations could ben resume like this: Sultân Veled, or more exactly Bahâ' al-Dîn Veled is the first son of the marriage of Rûmî with Gawhar Khâtûn, the daughter of Sharaf al-dîn, Lâlâ of Samarqand. The second son from the same wife was 'Alâ al-Dîn. After the death of Gawhar Khâtûn, Rûmî got married again, this time with Kirâ Khâtûn—herself a widow—who survived to Rûmî ninenteen years, leaving two other kids to the posterity, one of her first relation.[2] It is a matter of fact that exist many documents related with the early history of the Mevleviye, the mystical order inspired by Rûmî and organized by his son. The information held in the hagiographical life of Rûmî and the early history of the order are a vast field where emerge the image of Sultan's Valad's father and mostly the spiritual relation between them. The

1. For an introduction to the life of Rûmî and of his Sufi Order, see: AF Ambrosio, E Pierunek, and Th Zarcone, *Les derviches tourneurs. Doctrine, histoire et pratiques* (Paris: Les Editions du Cerf, 2006); Leili Anvar-Chenderoff, *Rûmî* (Paris: Editions Entrelacs, 2004); Franklin D Lewis, Franklin, *Rumi: Past and Present, East and West. The Life, Teaching and Poetry of Jalâl al-Din Rumi* (Oxford: Oneworld Publications, 2000); Gölpınarlı Abdülbâki, *Mevlânâ'dan sonra Mevlevilik* (Istanbul: İnkılâp ve Aka, 1982).
2. Ashk P Dahlén, 'Female Sufi Saints and Disciples: Women in the life of Jalāl al-dīn Rūmī', in *Orientalia Suecana*, LVII (2008): 46–62.

material is different in his approach and his intention: the difference that exists between the *Manaqib al-ʿarifin* of Shams al-dîn Ahmad Aflâkî and the *Valad-nâme*, Veled's one work, is quite evident for the historians, but maybe less for the reader who is trying to learn a spiritual lesson and the treatise of Sipehsâlâr.

The present paper is an enquiring of the first hand hagiographical material on the relation between Rûmî and his son Sultan Valad, and how this relation has been transmitted by the ottoman—mostly mevlevî—historiography. As a matter of fact, the family of Rûmî, the Çelebi, even if their origin is difficult to classify, is a family who spread out its spiritual and civil power firstly at the time of the Principalities and, only afterwards in the Ottoman Empire. They became in a certain way an Ottoman family, in spite of their origin, and a kind of spiritual *pendant* of the Empire household. Ekrem Işın, in an interesting paper which is more an analysis than a collection of information, asserted that in one way the Çelebi was the spiritual correspondent of the Ottoman household, but in another way, they were—for a long time—associated to the Principalities' power, and in this perspective, they were a part of a rival power. One of the sure indications is the fact the Mevleviye reached Istanbul, the capital of the Ottoman Empire, only after few decades from the Turkish conquest of the Byzantine Empire capital.[3] The origin as well the relation with the political power of the Rûmî' family could not been underestimated the Ottomans.

The present goal is the image of a father and his son—both mystics—as depicted by the Ottoman sources related with the Order's history. How the ottoman material has granted a transmission of a very deeply relation? Has the first image as depicted by the Persian sources been conserved by the follow ottoman authors?

After a presentation of some hagiographical materials, the analysis will be oriented to the evolution from the first image of the Sultan Veled related with his father, to the following representations.

3. Ekrem Işın, 'İstanbulda Mevlevi Şeyh aileleri ve Mevleviliğin bir imparatorluk tarikatı olarak örgütlenmesi', in *Birinci uluslararası Mevlana, mesnevi ve mevlevihaneler sempozyumu bildirileri [Uluslararası Mevlana Mesnevi ve Mevlevihaneler Sempozyumu (I : 2001 : Manisa)]*, edited by Küey Emrehan (Manisa: Celal Bayar Üniversitesi, 2002), 33–40.

The Persian sources of a family's *souvenirs*

The first history of the family of Rûmî is recorded especially in the *Manaqib al-ʿarifîn* of Shams al-Dîn Ahmed Aflâkî (m 1360),[4] but before it, the same Sultân Veled wrote the beginnings of the Mevlevîyye or, in his own words, the book of the son (*Valadnâme*). Both works, written in Farsi, are extremely important for the whirling dervishes' historiography as well for the relation between Rûmî and his son.

Speros Vryonis wrote, in 1993, a paper about the importance of the *Manaqib al-ʿarifîn* as a precious document for the cultural history of the Rûmî's time. He affirmed that 'Though Eflaki's work is hagiographical through and through, it is also an important and very interesting cultural document. Scholars have long been aware of this but have used it peripherally, preferring the important chronicles, waqfnames, and rich inscriptional materials'.[5] Vryonis inscribes his work in his research on the Anatolian culture in the Aflâkî's eyes. His article is on the situation of a Muslim family, that of Rûmî himself, but doesn't deal with the image of the relation between the father and Sultân Veled.

Muhammad Bahâ ad-Dîn Sultân Veled, the son of the Great Master is the third successor of the sufi order, the heir of the spirit of Rûmî, the one who follows the same path of the father. Son of Rûmî and of his second wife, Gowhar Khatun (m before 1229), Sultân Veled received the name of the 'son of the Sultân', because of his grandfather, the Sultân of the Ulama, and because of his mother who was one of the Princess of the Kharezm. In any case, the Aflâkî's work offers many interesting stimuli for going ahead in the enquiring. In this enormous work, one chapter is entirely devoted to the third *khalifa* of the *tarîqa* of the whirling dervishes, Sultân Veled.

Born approximately in 1226, Sultân Veled was about five when his grandfather Bahâ al-Dîn died and he was twenty when he

---

4. Shams al-Dîn Ahmad-e Aflâkî, *The Feats of the Knowers of God (Manâqeb al-ʿarefîn)*, translated by John O'Kane (Leiden: Brill, 2002), xxi, 788.

5. Vryonis, Speros, 'The Muslim Family in 13th-14th Century Anatolia as Reflected in the Writings of the Mawlawi Dervish Eflaki', in *Halcyon days in Crete I. A symposium held in Rethymnon 11-13 January 1991 The Ottoman Emirate 1300-1389 [Halcyon Days in Crete (1991 : Rethymnon (Crete)] The Ottoman Emirate (1300-1389)*, edited by E Zachariadou (Rethumnon: Crete University Press, 1993), 213–223, 214.

asked his father permission to do a retreat (*çelle*) for forty days. The hagiography of Aflâkî is rich in details about the tenderness and the relation between the father and the son, that stand as a pillar. Just after the birth of Sultân, Aflâkî writes that 'he continually slept in the arms of Mowlānā'[6] and just at the moment where Rûmî wanted to perform the prayer of the night, his son began to cry, so 'to make Valad calm down Mowlānā abandon the prayers and pick him up in his arms'.[7] Aflâkî registers an extremely interesting annotation of this paternal relation, that draws a very deep transmission of the spiritual power and the charisma:

> On occasions when he wanted his mother's milk, Mowlānā placed his own blessed nipple in Valad's month. By divine command, due to the extreme paternal kindness of: *clear milk, tasty to those who drink it*, pure milk would flow forth so that Valad would drink his fill (*sīr sīr*) of that lion (*shīr*) of higher meaning's milk (*shīr*), and go to sleep.[8]

The extreme paternal kindness is the certain sign that his destiny is to become his successor. At the age of ten, Sultân Valad is worthy to seat alongside his father during his spiritual instructions to his own disciples. Because of his wisdom, people thought that he was the Rûmî's brother. The spiritual communication is represented sometimes, as view before, in some surprising physical actions: 'It is said that he constantly put his blessed tongue in his mouth and would lick it. And he would plant kisses on his face and hair.'[9] The kiss by lips or in tongue is, especially in the Semitic culture, a tradition. Moses died after the God's kisses, it means after he received the Spirit of God.[10] The life of Sultân Veled seems to be shaped on the life of his father, in the sens that he follows as the best disciples the

6. Shams al-Dîn Ahmad-e Aflâkî, *The Feats of the Knowers of God (Manâqeb al-ʿarefîn)*, 547.
7. Shams al-Dîn Ahmad-e Aflâkî, *The Feats of the Knowers of God (Manâqeb al-ʿarefîn)*, 547.
8. Shams al-Dîn Ahmad-e Aflâkî, *The Feats of the Knowers of God (Manâqeb al-ʿarefîn)*, 547.
9. Shams al-Dîn Ahmad-e Aflâkî, *The Feats of the Knowers of God (Manâqeb al-ʿarefîn)*, 548.
10. Fishbane, Michael, *The Kiss of God: Spiritual and Mystical Deaht in Judaism*, (Washington DC : University of Washington Press, 1994).

path of Rûmî. Several passages of the Rûmî's hagiography by Aflâkî encourage through this interpretation of resembling of each other, like when Rûmî said to his son: 'Bahā' al-Dīn, my coming into this world for the sake of your appearance. For all these words of mine are my speech, whereas you are my action.'[11] The beloved son is the living speech of the father, the true successor of the familiar heritage. In fact, after this sentence, Aflâkî reports immediately below, the death of Rûmî and, especially, the question of the money collect for building his shrine. By the prayer of the son, Sultân Veled, obtains from the God the Higher, the support for this enterprise that should have immortalize the memory of the father. Again, after this, Aflâkî continues his way to depict the son like the father and, probably, to build up the hagiology of Sultân Veled. This one had, like the father, to perform a retreat of forty days and night, practicing the fast and the spiritual life. At the end: 'The revered father (*vāled*) saw the Valad (the son) was immersed in light and had taken on a wondrous appearance. When Valad beheld the blessed face of his father, he lowered his head and embraced his father's foot and for a long time kissed it and licked it.'[12] The relation between the Rûmî and the son is so special that there would be the temptation of a sexual metaphor for describing the union of aims and thoughts. As Mahdi Tourage has pointed out in his work the eroticism is an hermeneutic in the Rûmî's poetry and, it is not at all surprising, if the same hermeneutic has begun to use by the first time of the hagiography and the mevlevî historiography.[13] The humble devotion of the son regarding the father is, as before seen, showed by the action—that is probably a true sufi ritual—of bowing the head till the father's head and embracing the feet.[14] This is the paradoxical humility that links the lowest member of the body, the feet, and the highest part of it, the head. The hermeneutical circle is

11. Shams al-Dîn Ahmad-e Aflâkî, *The Feats of the Knowers of God (Manâqeb al-'arefîn)*, 552.

12. Shams al-Dîn Ahmad-e Aflâkî, *The Feats of the Knowers of God (Manâqeb al-'arefîn)*, 554.

13. Tourage, Mahdi, *Rūmī and the Hermeneutics of Eroticism* (Leiden/Boston: Brill, 2007).

14. 'Valad immediately dismounted and placed his head on Mowlānā's foot and sought forgiveness', 'Valad lowered his head and planted kisses on his father's blessed foot', Shams al-Dîn Ahmad-e Aflâkî, *The Feats of the Knowers of God (Manâqeb al-'arefîn)*, 559.

also represented by this gesture of humility where the highest reaches the lowest, the intelligence bows face to the dust.

Sultân Veled had also a special mission from his father. When Shams al-Dîn Tabrîzî left Konya, because the latter was suspected by the Rûmî's entourage to corrupt the Great Master, Sultân Veled departed in quest of the mirror of Rûmî. In 1246, Sultân Veled reached Damascus to find his father's spiritual master. What he did with success and Shams came back to Konya for a second period that will be meet an end some time later.

The aim of the father was as well as to do of his son a disciple of the same master: 'When Mowlānā made Valad a disciple of Mowlānā Shams al-Dīn-e Tabrīzī—*God sanctify their innermost secret*—he sad: "My Bahā al-Dīn dies bit eat hashish and never commits sodomy, because *in the eyes of God the Generous* these two practices are highly uncommendable and blameworthy".'[15] If in a way, this sentence risks to confirm exactly what Rûmî is trying to criticize, it says also his concern of proposing Shams as the model, because this one was the master of the father. The model for everything was the son, in a certain way and according to the hagiographer, resemble to the father.

After the death of Rûmî, the Order was directed by Salah ad-Dîn Zarkubî (d 1258), first, and after the Zarkubî's death by Husâm ad-Dîn Chalabi (d 1284). When Salâh al-Dîn Zarkûbî, the second spiritual guide of the Great Master, died, Rûmî's son was thirty-two and when his own father left this world, he was forty-two. At the moment of the death of Hosâm al-Dîn, the disciples of the mystical Way asked to Sultân Veled to be their new guide. At the time, Veled was forty-seven and he felt a heard responsibility and his incapacity to carry on the Order. One night, he received the visit, in a dream, of Husâm al-Dîn who encouraged him to go ahead in the path of the direction of the Way.[16] Only after this two prominent personalities, Sultân Veled, in a special humble way, accepted the task to carry on the new mystical way of his father. Aflâkî related also that one day, Rûmî was sitting in the blessed Madrasa of Konya and his sons were sitting on his sides: Sultân Veled on his right and 'Alâ' al-Dîn on his left. Suddenly two persons came from the invisible world and, after greeting Rûmî, took

15. Shams al-Dîn Ahmad-e Aflâkî, *The Feats of the Knowers of God (Manâqeb al-'arefîn)*, 436.

16. Lewis, Franklin D., *Rumi: Past and Present, East and West. The Life, Teaching and Poetry of Jalâl al-Din Rumi* (Oxford : Oneworld Publications, 2000), 230–237.

Valad by the hand and departed. After a while, the came back to take the Veled's son and departed. While 'Alâ al-Dîn was wounded and died, Sultân Veled was left in this world for a reason that his father himself revealed to his disciples: 'This son is required by human beings for the procreation of Bahā'-e Valad's progeny-*God sanctify his innermost secret*!.'[17] Aflâkî adds that, after Rûmî's death, Sultân Veled lived on in tranquillity, writing three spiritual books and one volume of poems and pursues telling that:

> He filled the world with divine insights, higher truths and wondrous secrets, and transformed many thick-headed fools into learned knowers of God and effective religious scholars. And he clarified and explained all his father's words by means of wondrous parables and incomparable similitudes. Indeed, Solṭān Valad was the secret cause of the arrival of this *ḥadīth* from the Prophet: 'The son (*valad*) is the secret of the father'.[18]

Sultân Veled is thus the secret of Rûmî and in this perspective, his own essence. Following him, the disciples are sure that they are in the right way of the Great Master. Even before his death, Husâm al-Dîn, the second successor in the mevlevî Order, confirmed Veled and supported him with some words that sound like an official sufi investiture, by the uwaysî way. In fact, Husâm al-Dîn, giving his advices to the Veled who was in a state of personal anxiety and sorrow with the perspective to carry on the birthing mevlevî sufi Order, encourage him with his hereafter worldly support:

> After my death whenever you are confronted with a task and an important matter and a difficulty and a knot with you cannot deal with, I will come before you in another appearance and present myself to you. I will take on the form of a luminous body and manifest myself in various rays of light so that your difficulties will be resolved and the knots will be undone and you will have need of no one else [...] Know that in reality every form which comes before you to give you spiritual guidance is I and none other than I and belongs to no one but me. Likewise,

17. Shams al-Dîn Ahmad-e Aflâkî, *The Feats of the Knowers of God (Manâqeb al-'arefîn)*, 561.
18. Shams al-Dîn Ahmad-e Aflâkî, *The Feats of the Knowers of God (Manâqeb al-'arefîn)*, 561.

> at times I will reveal myself to you in a dream and you will attain your religious and wordly goals through me.[19]

In this seventh chapter of the Aflâkî's hagiography of Rûmî that is worth to a deeper study in a textual point of view, there is an astonishing theme that recurs some times and already mentioned. It is what it could be named the face-to-face of the father and the son. While Rûmî, the father, had very pale complexion, according to a report of the Pervâna, the minister, the son had is very rose-faced. The query is why the son is rosy-faced unlike the father, because he is supposed to have even the same physical facial characters. The answer was done immediately: 'Valad, from the moment of his birth, was a beloved, and beloveds possess a rosy hue and lips like Yemeni cornelian.'[20] The beloveds are signed by a uncontroversial sign that everyone can recognize without any difficult. In fact, just in the following paragraph, Aflâkî, comes back to the same topic and a reports a fact that is more fascinating and interesting for the relationship between both personalities. Valad himself records:

> In the realm of youth it happened to me that I did not see my father's face for several days and I was overcome with longing for him. Suddenly he summoned me. I went before him and lowered my head. From within extreme spiritual immersion he gazed at me passionately with an awesome look so that I lost my senses and my father too lost his self-control. Then he gazed at me again with an awesome look and again he lost his self-control. After a moment, he gazed at me a third time with a look of mercy in such a way that I beheld myself completely eradicated and non-existent.[21]

In the hagiography, of course, Rûmî gave three reasons of his consciousness, religious and spiritual at the same time. But the interpretation of Veled appears more meaningfully: 'The royal crown he saw placed on top of my head is in fact the shadow of his favor

19. Shams al-Dîn Ahmad-e Aflâkî, *The Feats of the Knowers of God (Manâqeb al-'arefîn)*, 564.
20. Shams al-Dîn Ahmad-e Aflâkî, *The Feats of the Knowers of God (Manâqeb al-'arefîn)*, 568.
21. Shams al-Dîn Ahmad-e Aflâkî, *The Feats of the Knowers of God (Manâqeb al-'arefîn)*, 569.

over my head. And the ear-ring bearing a single pearl which he saw hanging from my ear is the innermost secret of our Jalāl al-Dīn 'Aref who came into being from me.'[22] The secret of the son is recorded in the father and the face is the living evidence of this identity.

Resuming some points concerning Sultân Veled recorded in the hagiography of Rûmî written by Aflâkî, the main aim of the author is in order to create a true continuity between the father and the son, in physical sense as well in spiritual terms. The sufi Order, the Mevleviye, could not have been carried on by a different personality. The length is a mark of religious fidelity to the charisma and the reliability for the disciples. In fact, a sufi Order can keep its own mission just if its members can to stand on the reality of spiritual permanence. The stability is represented by the oneness of mystical witness. In this same point of view, the fact that Sultân Veled, in his own books, borrowed a lot of Rûmî's poems without quoting the author—means the father—is a clear sign of this will of showing just one reality. The family is sanctified by the Great master, the father, but all members of the family fell a kind of shared charisma. At least, we can say that Aflâkî and his masterpiece of hagiography do it.

Sultân Veled, in his own work of the beginnings, says that after Husâm ad-Dîn, for seven years, Kerim ad-Dîn, directed the Way. At the opposite, Aflâkî himself tells that the successor was Husâm ad-Dîn,[23] without any information about Kerim ad-Dîn, except a quotation of him as high personality worth of respect and consideration. Rûmî, after the wise words pronounced by Kerim

22. Shams al-Dîn Ahmad-e Aflâkî, *The Feats of the Knowers of God (Manâqeb al-'arefîn)*, 570.

23. Sultân Walad, *Ibditâ-nâme* (Tahran: Khorezmî, 1389), 312; Sultan Veled, Bahaeddin Muhammed Veled, *İbtida - name*, turkish version by Abdülbaki Gölpınarlı (Konya: Konya Turizm Derneği, 1976), 316; Sultan Valad, *La parole secrète: l'enseignement du maître soufi Rûmî*, translation by Eva de Vitray-Meyerovitch, (Paris, Sindbad, 1982), 236; Küçük, Hülya, 'Sultan Veled'in İbtida-Name'sine göre Mevlevi Halifeleri/The Caliphs of Mevlevi According to İbtidaname's Sultan Walad', in 3. *Uluslararası Mevlana Kongresi/3rd International Mevlana Congress: Bildiriler*, edited by Nuri Şimşekler (Konya: Selçuk Üniversitesi, 2004), 85–94; Önder, Mehmet, « Mevlevîliğin Sistemleşmesi, Sultan Veled ve Diğer Postnişînler », in *Konya'dan Dünya'ya Mevlâna ve Mevlevîlik*, edited by Nuri Şimsekler (Karatay: Belediyesi, 2002), 131–150.

ad-Dîn, replied: 'This thought is not found written in any book.'[24] Aflâkî offered to his readers just this reference to Kerim ad-Dîn, who, in the eyes of Sultân Veled and Sipehsâlâr, could be one of the spiritual master of the Mevleviye, after the Rûmî's death. In the hagiography's point of view, the treatise of Sipehsâlâr is also worthy of consideration. Sipehsâlâr (fourteenth century) is one of the companions of the Mevleviye Order a century after the Rûmî's death. He did not probably personally meet Rûmî and so that the images of the very first paths of the mevlevî dervishes are recorded by the transmission of the souvenirs of sayings. Himself writes the Rûmî's life leaving a chapter to his son, but it is totally different in the shape and in the style from the Aflâkî's one. The tenderness and the feelings tieying each other are not anymore recorded. The image of Sultân Veled that comes out from the pages of Sipehsâlâr's treatise is—this time is the case—very pale. All the Rûmî's hagiography of Sipehsâlâr is concentrated on his mystical personality of the founder. The biography is more a hagiography than a work between the history and the interpretation of a spiritual story. A century after the father's death, the idealistic construction of the Rûmî's family power is probably or certainly well established. The Çelebi is now an almost official institution in the religious context and even in the relations with the political power. They don't need anymore to resort to a ideal construction of the spiritual power of the family. In a certain way, this is already a matter of fact and the Mevleviye can concentrate its efforts of understanding of the charisma on the Great Master, Rûmî.

On the other hand, Sipehsâlâr can add the Veled's progeny that Aflâkî was only able to imagine. The follower of Veled are four, at the time where the author of the treatise is writing: Çelebi 'Arif, Çelebi 'Âbid, Çelebi Zâhid and the last Çelebi Wâjid.[25] As a matter of fact, the family's members are all Çelebi, word meaning in general illustrious but giving also an idea of the divine. From that time on, Rûmî's descendants are the Great Masters of the Mevleviye, and they represent that this Sufi Order is family oriented in the spiritual and

24. Shams al-Dîn Ahmad-e Aflâkî, *The Feats of the Knowers of God (Manâqeb al-'arefîn)*, 123.

25. Faridûn b Ahmad Sipahsâlâr, *Risâlah Sipahsâlâr dar manâqib-i hazrat-i khodâvandgâr*, edited by M Afshin Vafâie (Tahran: Sukhan, 2006), 126.

political government. Sipehsâlâr, just after giving the successors as masters, records the death of the Rûmî's son. This report is interesting by different points of view. Çelebi 'Arif, his first son, invited his friends and his disciples as well the Shams' disciples for surrounding him during the last hours of his life, but he didn't let the others—meaning the people outside the spiritual circle—stay alongside his sickbed.[26] This details are of extreme importance because from one side, only the disciples of Veled and Shams were admitted by the Çelebi 'Arif, his son. On the other side, we exactly know that at that time, two currents were explicitly exiting: the Veled's branch and the Shams' branch of the Mevleviye. If this hypothesis was rejected—that some scholars are doing—the question should have stand on. Why did Sipehsâlâr feel the need to write that there are two orders of disciples: the one of Veled and the others of Shams. And again: why did Sipehsâlâr write the exclusion of the stranger people around the Veled's house, while his father's burial report was a triumph of attendance of people from different religious community living in Konya? Has the perspective changed entirely? It is quite probably that disciples of Rûmî must keep the charisma of the Great Master for their own circle, before sharing it with other. In any case, Veled's death registers a different hagiographical orientation. At the end of the story, few pages reveal more than we can imagine before analyzing them, because these two details are so important. One century after the founder's death, the Sufi Order of Mevlevîs shows different trends in terms of religious path and rituals. The relation existed between Rûmî and his son, is—in the eyes of Sipehsâlâr—more pale in its familiar feelings, shared thoughts and poetry and even in similarity of face, but the element well established is the policy of the piety. Sipehsâlâr is more aware of the trends of the Mevleviye and he has to preserve the nuances of approaches as well as the unity of the Sufi Order. This seems to be a worry political as well spiritual, simple understandable if we think that the member of the Rûmî's family is the successor of a great and more and more important Order.

---

26. Faridûn b Ahmad Sipahsâlâr, *Risâlah Sipahsâlâr dar manâqib-i hazrat-i khodâvandgâr*, 126.

Between Ottoman hagiography and historiography

If two other Persian sources, the *Nefahat al-Uns* of 'Abd al-Rahmân Jâmî (d 1492) and the *Tezkire-i şuara* of Devletşâh (d 1495), do not offer any information about the relation between the father and the son, the Ottoman sources are neither abundant. From the Aflâkî's point of view, the approach seems to change remarkably. The Ottoman hagiography still need a deep enquiry and a full study for exploiting successfully the richness of the texts. In this way, the Rûmî and Mevleviye's Ottoman sources are studied firstly by the Turkish scholars, but mostly in a theological point of view. As Ahmet Yaşar Ocak had pointed out since few decades, the Ottoman sufi literature, and mostly the hagiography, still a different and more critical approach.[27] In this respect, the Ottoman hagiography of Rûmî are a lack in the mevlevî panorama, even if the general interest is increasing and giving more and more results.[28] Still today, no one study has been consecrated to compare the Ottoman translation of the Persian materials, nor they have not published yet. In this case, it is very difficult to say what of Persian memory of the Mevleviye has passed into Ottoman. With the available materials, we can guess—probably with a good average of truth—the transformation of the historiography.

The first hagiography in ottoman, the *Menâkib-i Mevlânâ* of a mevlevî author Lokmânî Dede (d 1519), gives some verses about Sultân Veled.[29] The work of Lokmânî who was in charge for the shrine of Rûmî in Konya, is the result of a mix between the important two hagiographies in persian. Lokmânî saw in a dream that he had to write the life of his Great Master and he decided and, after his effort to compose in verses his Rûmî's biography dedicated the work to the Sultân Bayazid the second. Instead of the 4428 double verses in ancient

27. Ocak Yaşar, Ahmet, 'Türkiye'de 1980 Sonrası Tasavvuf tarihi araştırmalarına genel bir bakış', *Toplumsal Tarih*, 2002/108, pp. 10-19; *id.*, *Kültür tarihi Kaynağı olarak Menâkıbnameler (Metodolojik Bir Yaklaşım)*, (Ankara: Türk Tarih Kurumu Basımevi, 1992).
28. Öztürkmen, Arzu, 'Orality and Performance in Late Medieval Turkish Texts: Epic Tales, Hagiographies, and Chronicles', in *Text and Performance Quarterly*, 29 (2009): 327–345; Bayram, Fatih, '*A Sufi Saint accross Centuries : The Analysis of the Makalat-i Seyyid Harun*', in *Turcica*, 40 (2008): 7–36.
29. Lokmâni Dede, *Menâkıb-i Mevlânâ*, edited by Halil Ersoylu (Ankara: Türk Dil Kurumu Yayınları, 2001).

Ottoman language, with several quotation of poems in Persian, very few times, Lokmânî stopped on the Veled relation with his father. Of course, he recorded that 'the Servant of the Saints, Jalâl al-Dîn/his son was Veled Bahâ' al-Dîn'.[30] And immediately after, he quotes the successors of Rûmî, Salah al-Dîn and Husâm al-Dîn without adding anything else. Lokmânî depicts Veled as one who knew the spiritual stations and wrote on them with science and personal experience. He knew the secret and the inner life and, as Lokmânî affirms, 'Shams and Molla Veled were the same/together they were patient and passionnated'.[31] This identity of Shams and Veled is quite surprising and one of the reasons for understanding it is to remind the risk of division of the one Mevleviye in to two branches. The fourteenth century author say clearly that Shams and Veled were the light of the two worlds: 'Shams and the Molla of the Rûm's country, Sultân Veled/for ever and never they were the light of the world.'[32] Veled is more related to the personality of Shams, he is his disciple and so that he was plenty of wisdom: 'Sultân Veled became Shams' disciple/ his heart and soul were fulfilled by wisdom.'[33] The relation between Shams and Veled is depicted by Lokmânî as almost secret, by talking both exchanged the truths of inner life: 'Shams with the Molla Sultân Veled/were used to talk secretly'.[34] On the path of Rûmî, Lokmânî knows exactly that after Veled came his son, but the way of writing down the succession is also a sign of a different perception: 'Or the one like Sultan Veled come!/Also like is son will he come?'[35] Another element in the poem of Lokmânî describes Veled and his father like a symbol with the passionate love, that means a religious sign for the world: 'Look at Molla with Sultan Veled/A symbol with the passionate love, how they are a sign!'[36] Through the end of the hagiography in verses, Lokmânî affirms also that Veled and his son were the knowers of the Love: 'The Prince Sultân Veled and 'Ârif/were knowers of the love with heart and soul.'[37]

30. Lokmâni Dede, *Menâkıb-i Mevlânâ*, 80, vv. 779–780.
31. Lokmâni Dede, *Menâkıb-i Mevlânâ*, 167, vv. 1588–1589
32. Lokmâni Dede, *Menâkıb-i Mevlânâ*, 189, vv. 1752-1753.
33. Lokmâni Dede, *Menâkıb-i Mevlânâ*, 172, vv. 1627-1628.
34. Lokmâni Dede, *Menâkıb-i Mevlânâ*, 175, vv. 1658-1659
35. Lokmâni Dede, *Menâkıb-i Mevlânâ*, 239, vv. 2183-2184.
36. Lokmâni Dede, *Menâkıb-i Mevlânâ*, 263, vv. 2393-2394.
37. Lokmâni Dede, *Menâkıb-i Mevlânâ*, 470, vv. 4357-4358.

Finally, the hagiography of Lokmânî does not record the tenderness of Rûmî and Veled as depicted in Aflâkî, nor the approach used in the treatise of Sipehsâlâr, but shows the idea of a Veled very close to Shams, keeping probably the secrets of Rûmî. This remark needs to be compared, in a second time, with a recognition of the Aflâkî's *Manaqib al-'arifîn*: it is not certain that some reports where the author stresses the tenderness and the very special relation between the father and the son, are translated. The transmission of a puritan hagiography is probably the base for the new Ottoman historiography with regard to the Mevleviye. Sultân Veled is, first of all, the successor of the Rûmî's family line.

The translation of the Trabzonlu Köseç Ahmet Dede (d 1777) *Et-Tuhfetü'l-behiyye fi't-Tarikati'l-Mevlevîyye Tercümesi (Zâviye-i fukarâ)* by one of the latest mevlevî, Ahmet Remzi Akyürek (d 1944), offers to the readers some parts as regard with Rûmî and his son.[38] In this eighteenth work, translated in a recent age, there is the attention to record a relation more familiar, even if the general sensibility is more oriented to preserve the main carachter of the story: affirm the continuity between the father and the son. Some spiritual sentences are still dedicated to the filial attention.

The more historical works of the Mevleviye, for consequence, as *Sefine-i nefîse-i Mevleviyân* of Sâkıb Mustafa Dede (d 1735) bypasses the time of the foundation of the Sufi Order.[39] In this case, any information about Rûmî and his son has not given for the reader. The reference book, at the Sâkıb Mustafa's age was the Aflâkî's hagiography as well the different ottoman translation of the same work. A following Ottoman historical writing concerning the mevlevî Order is the *Mecmuatü't-Tevarîhi'l-Mevleviye* of the mevlevî author Sahîh Ahmed Dede (d 1813).[40] The last one says few words about Veled, more than the Lokmânî's hagiography, but in terms of familial relationship the information are very poor.

In one of the lastest biography of Rûmî, at the end of the Ottoman Empire, the personality of Sultân Veled is even not mentioned. It is

38. Trabzonlu Köseç Ahmet Dede, *Et-Tuhfetü'l-behiyye fi't-Tarikati'l-Mevlevîyye Tercümesi (Zâviye-i fukarâ). Mevlevîlik Âdâbı, Anektodlar*, haz. Ali Üremiş (Trabzon: Serander, 2008), 76–100.

39. Sâkıb Dede, *Sefine-i nefîse-i Mevleviyân* (Le Caire): Bulaq, 1283/1866-67.

40. Seyyin Ahmed Dede, *Mevlevîlerin Tarihi. Mecmûatü't-Tevârîhi'l-Mevleviyye*, edited by Cem Zorlu (Istanbul: İnsan yayınları, 2003).

quite surprising that an author as Osman Behçet did not even quote the names of the sons of the mystical philosopher of Konya.[41] Another important work of the end of Ottoman Empire, the *Sefîne-i Evliyâ*, leaves a short chapter to the second successor of the Mevleviye and any kind of information about the feelings intercourse between are not mentioned.[42]

Browsing the Ottoman literature of different style (hagiography, historical records, poems and biography), the most influent fact that is recorded is the fact that Sultân Veled was the intermediary between Rûmî's entourage and Shams, the unruly friend of God, in the periods of controversy. As mentioned before, Shams was the prey of the circle of the Great Master. Fuat Köprülü (d 1966), a Turkish scholar who lived the passage from the end of Ottoman Empire and the Turkish Republic era, granted a kind of Turkishness of the Turkish Sufi studies' approach. In his masterpiece, he quotes Sultân Veled, stressed that he left some poems in Turkish, but does a syntheses that, in its simplicity, depicts a real character existing since the Aflâkî's time. Koprülü affirms that:

> Sulṭān Walad, who desired nothing more than to propagate the Ṣūfī principles that his father had put forward, and whose personality therefore never emerges as distinct from that of his father, tried to compose in Turkish according to the examples of Persian Ṣūfī literature. Mawlānā's influence on Turkish poetry, just as it was in composing and reciting Persian poetry, was to raise the religious consciousness of the people of Anatolia, to guide them, and instill in them a sense of the greatness of Mawlānā.[43]

Fuat Köprülü also says the dependence of Sultân Veled to his father, and he says the truth with regard to the first sources, but he doesn't mention anymore the familiar feelings that seem to be constitutive in the Persian records.

---

41. Osman Behçet (Kadıköy Sultânîsi muallimlerinden), *Mevlâna Celâleddin Rûmî Hayatı ve Yolu*, ed. Dilaver Gürer (Konya: Rûmî Yayınları, 2007), 62.
42. Osmânzâde Hüseyin Vassâf, *Sefîne-i Evliyâ*, ed. Mehmet Akkuş and Ali Yılmaz, (Istanbul: Kitabevi, 2006), volume 1, 388–389.
43. Köprülü, Mehmed Fuad *Early Mistics in Turkish Literature*, edited by Robert Dankoff and Gary Leiser, (London/New York: Routledge, 2006), 208.

The samples taken by the Ottoman texts lead the readers to a more official interpretation of the relation between Rûmî and his son. The non-homogenous texts analyzed allow to affirm, at least, the Ottoman tradition is switching from a hagiography whom field is very large to an official ideology, that could be as well the mevlevî historiography. The Ottomans are more interested in focusing on the continuity of the Sufi Order than a picture of a circle. We can assert somehow that the Ottoman tradition is being impoverished by the maintain of the doctrine, the organization of the Order and the foundation of the silsile. This is the core of the question. Sultân Veled is finally the Rûmî's family member and, in the name of this relationship founded on the blood, is the Great Master, the successor of Rûmî.[44]

Conclusion

The digression might appear too rapid in terms of materials studied and natures of the texts. The difference of historical and political context is not been underestimated, because from the Seljuk time to the Ottoman and the late Ottoman Empire Era the sufi understanding of the Orders organization is more important than the thirteenth century. The Sufi Order's self-perception, rituals and structure represent the aim of the mystical path. In this perspective, it is not surprising that the Rûmî and his son Sultân Veled's relation is depicted differently through the ages. From a tenderness of the first time, a tenderness that can become even suspect in some records, the Ottoman tradition seems to impoverish this representation of the family feelings, for giving more importance to the legal status of the son. Sultân Veled is the one, in the family, who had succeeded in take back the right of succession in the Mevleviye's Order. It is a turning point. Aflâkî recorded this important passage in the lineage of the sufi Order. During the centuries, especially the Ottoman time, the writers—mostly if mevlevî—and the other—like an ottoman reflex—set apart the very tender feelings depicted by Aflâkî, the spiritual identity for focusing themselves on the continuity of the family tradition. We assist, for consequence, to the foundation of the Çelebi's

44. Işın, Ekrem, 'Mevleviliğin Tarihsel Temelleri: Sultan Veled ve Çelebilik Makamının Kuruluşu', in *3. Uluslararası Mevlana Kongresi/3rd International Mevlana Congress : Bildiriler*, edited by Nuri Şimşekler, (Konya: Selçuk Üniversitesi, 2004), 95–98.

power. In fact, the Ottoman tradition affirms an identity between the father and the son and, in this regard, the Persian source of Aflâkî seems to follow the same spiritual procedure. But, in an another point of view, aside the identity of the father and the son in the Aflâkî's work, we find also the feelings, very deep, the idea the son is the secret of the father, because he received from him. The transmission has created somehow a new master and the reader can not forget it. The lost of the family feelings along the centuries, mostly in the written texts more than oral transmitted records, lead to a symptomatic conclusion on the nature of spiritual identity. Losing the family's feeling for setting the authoritative and spiritual law of the succession and inheritance means adopting a more official hermeneutic and less mystical. The Ottoman tradition lost in a mystic of the family elements in order to found the authoritative succession on the family lineage.

The Castle of God is the Centre of the Dervish's Soul

History and Symbols of a Mystical Order

In any conversation about dervishes, one thinks immediately of the ritual of *Samāʿ* (Turkish: *sema*), the dervishes' audition to music and the dance ceremony that defines them by typical movements—in particular the spinning of the 'whirling dervishes' practised by the Mevlevî Sufi order.[1] The Western and especially the European mind has often singled out this ritual of music and dance as being the main characteristic of Sufi dervishes, the visual expression of their spirituality—omitting all mention of their other spiritual practices. Since the seventeenth century, European travellers have debated the significance of the Sufi *samāʿ* ritual, describing in exotic detail the ecstasy that exhausted these men, usually considering it to be a bit 'weird'. In addition to *Samāʿ*, another practice that was often featured in European travel accounts and in the written records left by Christian missionaries sent to the eastern districts of Anatolia was the extraordinary hospitality shown by the Mevlevî to visitors to their lodges.

1. See A Ambrosio, È Feuillebois-Pierunek and Th Zarcone, *Les derviches tourneurs: doctrine, histoire et pratiques* (Paris: Les Editions du Cerf 2006); Sezai Küçük, *Mevlevîliğin Son Yüzyılı* (Istanbul: Simurg 2003); Victoria Rowe Holbrook, 'Diverse Tastes in the Spiritual Life: Textual Play in the Diffusion of Rumi's Order', in L Lewisohn, editor, *The Heritage of Sufism*: I: *The Legacy of Mediæval Persian Sufism*, (Oxford: Oneworld 1999), 99–120; Franklin D Lewis, *Rumi, Past and Present, East and West: the Life, Teaching and Poetry of Jalāl al-Dīn Rūmī*, (Oxford: Oneworld Publications 2000); Abdülbâki Gölpınarlı, *Mevlânâ'dan sonra Mevlevilik* (Istanbul: İnkılâp ve Aka), 1982.

And yet, the existence of recorded observations and study made by European travellers of this Sufi practice that has maintained its charm and its highly symbolic content over the centuries, does not necessarily render the task of the researcher any easier. Sometimes considered folklore, sometimes an attraction fit only for tourists, but at all times exotic, the *Samā'* ceremony of the Mevlevî order was, in fact, an epiphenomenon of various esoteric disciplines and the outcome of a religious initiation that took several years. Thus, another key Mevlevî spiritual practice was the retreat into a tiny cell (Persian: *chilla;* Turkish: *çile*), which lasted for a period of 1001 days, after which the postulate was elevated to his new status of as a Mevlevî dervish. These and many other lesser-known Sufi practices and rituals formed the substructure of Mevlevî contemplative disciplines. Self-control and the regulation of all aspects of everyday life under the auspices of the Muslim Sufi tradition represented the religious horizon of the Mevlevî Sufi's existence.

However, due to the political events which occurred in the early twentieth century, we must use the past tense in all discussion today of Mevlevî practices and rituals. The Mevlevî tradition, like others, was dismantled by an Act of the Turkish Parliament at the end of 1925.[2] Two years after the ratification of the constitution of the Republic of Turkey, a new religious policy that had no precedent in Ottoman history divested the Sufi Orders (*ṭarīqat*) and the Sufis of all legal right to exist. One can find evidence of a possibly similar religious politics in the edict of the Ottoman Sultan in 1666 which prohibited the practice of *Samā'*. The law promulgated by the newly formed Turkish Republic outlawed all the mystical brotherhoods and declared that all Sufi practices were henceforth to be considered as superstitious magical rituals that would be forever banned from Turkey's modern secular society. The Mevlevî Order, queen of the Sufi Orders in the Ottoman Empire, was thus bequeathed a historical transformation that would only become revealed over the following decades.[3]

2. Rabia Harmanşah, 'Ṭarīqatların Yasaklanması ve Sonrasında Mevleviler', in *Uluslararası düşünce ve Sanatta Mevlâna Sempozyumu Bildirileri. International Symposium on Mawlana Jalaladdin Rumi in Thought and Art Papers* (Konya: Rûmî Yayınları 2006), 589–97.
3. Hülya Küçük, *The Role of Bektashis in Turkey's National Struggle* (Leiden: Brill 2002); John Kingsley Birge, *The Bektashi Order of Dervishes* (London: Luzac & Co 1994) (1st ed. 1937); Ahmed Karamustafa, *Metinlerle Günümüz tasavvuf hareketleri (1839 - 2000)* (Istanbul: Dergâh Yayınları 2002), 147.

It is necessary to keep this political background in mind when approaching the study of the Mevlevî Order, since contemporary study of the Mevlevîye amounts to the study of a mystical order that was eventually consigned to history. Albeit, the living vitality of the Order one can still find revealed in manuscripts preserved in the best libraries of Turkey—or in other countries or archives—and even in the collective memory of persons and places that once hosted generations of Mevlevî mystics. In sum, despite appearances, Mevlevî history still remains very rich in terms of its literature, art, architecture, and its historical memories of life once lived and now remembered.

This contribution therefore belongs both to the field of the religious history of the Ottoman Empire, and to the interpretation of Sufi practices which can be extracted from the study of texts—texts which preserve, for all those who aspire to a rebirth of the brotherhood, the memory of living Sufi rituals and practices.

The memory of the central Mevlevî Sufi practice of invocation of God in the heart (Persian: *dhikr;* Turkish: *zikr*) has been deleted from the priorities of both the mystical and scholarly study of *Samā*ʿ. Although in some texts, *Samā*ʿ is itself treated as *dhikr*, that is, interpreted as a kind of remembrance of God and the divine attributes, the classical texts of the Mevlevî tradition also dealt separately with the subject of recollection of the sublime name of God. As is well-known, *dhikr/ zikr* is the central practice of Sufism. It consists of the continuous repetition of one of God's Names. Every Sufi disciple and every Mevlevî novice received from his spiritual master instruction in the techniques of contemplation and meditation on one of the ninety-nine beautiful names of God. *Dhikr* may be practised in the company of other dervishes or individually in private, repeated silently in the heart or vocalized aloud; it can also be practised both singly or in association with other names of God. In short, the varieties of this practice are as many as the different *ṭarīqat*s that exist. But the Mevlevî Order chose from among the many divine Names usually only one of these names—Allah, considered to be the sublime Name of God (Persian: *ism-i jalāl;* Turkish: *ism-i celal*)—and *dhikr* became synonymous in later Mevlevî tradition with the invocation of this Name.

The repetition of Allah, literally meaning 'the God', leads the Sufi to enter into the deepest reaches of the remembrance of God. As defined by Ismāʿil Ankaravī (d 1041/1631)—a leading Shaykh of the

Mevlevî convent (*Tekke*) in the Galata district located in the European quarter of Istanbul, and also one of the spiritual authorities who most influenced the interpretation of the Mevlevî ritual—the *dhikr* should understood to be a veritable 'castle of God'. In the third chapter of his treatise *Minhâcü'l-Fukarâ* (Persian: *Minhāj al-fuqarā'*, meaning: *A Manual for the Dervish Brethren*), Ankaravī deals with the secrets and virtues inherent in the practice of repeating the great name of Allah. There are two points in this essay that merit analysis: the metaphor of the castle and the ritual techniques concerning the Mevlevî *dhikr*.

The Castle of God: the Sufi's Sacred Space

Ankaravī's metaphor of the castle itself merit further consideration especially for its implications regarding mystical symbols, doctrines and rites found in other spiritual traditions.[4] Indeed, how can one not read in Ankaravī's definition of *dhikr* as the Castle of God (Turkish: *Hisn-i huda;* Persian: *Ḥiṣn-i khudā*) a reference to the 'Interior Castle'[5] of the Catholic Carmelite Saint Teresa of Avila?[6] In this regard, the works of Asin Palacios and Luce López-Baralt discerned a clear Islamic influence in Teresa's metaphor, arguing cogently that the interior castle, before becoming an image of the life of the Spirit, was originally a metaphor developed in the context of Muslim Sufi mysticism. Albeit, while López-Baralt never presents any incontrovertible opinion regarding the possibility of an Islamic influence on the development of the metaphor, her propensity for this assumption is explicit throughout her writings.[7]

The study of the origin of the Islamic symbol of Teresa's interior castle has its own historiography. Without going into the complexity of the debate, it is worth remembering here that there are different interpretations of the genesis of her image of the castle. In the early twentieth century, the great Spanish philosopher Miguel de Unamuno

4. Giovanni Tani, *Il castello interiore di santa Teresa d'Avila. Un'interpretazione simbolica* (Milan: San Paolo Edizioni 1991).
5. Santa Teresa de Jesus (1515–1582), *Obras completes* (Madrid: Editorial de Espiritualidad 1963).
6. Tomás Alvarez, 'Thérèse de Jésus (Sainte)', in *Dictionnaire de Spiritualité* (Paris: Beauchesne 1991), volume XV, coll 611–58.
7. See especially her *San Juan de la Cruz y el Islam: Estudio sobre las filiaciones semíticas de su literatura mística* (Puerto Rico: El Colegio de México 1985).

suggested that the idea of the castle had come to Teresa by the presence of a castle in the city of Avila. It is clear that the architecture that offers itself to the eye cannot remain without effect on the saint. Robert Ricard[8] and Trueman Dicken[9] a few decades later reaffirmed the validity of Unamuno's conjecture; Dicken even stated that it was the actual castle at Medina del Campo that offered to her a metaphor for the interior architecture of the castle. However, this hypothesis of an influence on Teresa's architecture of mysticism never convinced other scholars who focused more closely on the texts themselves.[10] Luce López-Baralt, a Puerto Rican scholar, followed Asín Palacios who had identified the presence of a description of the interior castle found in a compilation of stories in an Arabic work entitled *Nawādir* attributed to Aḥmad al-Qalyūbī. The author of *Nawādir* describes the journey through different castles made of precious materials, through which the human soul progresses on the path of divine contemplation. The last castle of gold encloses the contemplation of God.[11] López-Baralt went even further in tracing the derivation of the symbol from Arabic mystical literature. If the document used by Palacios could not confirm a precise literary transmission—the text dates, in fact, only to the sixteenth century—other texts ignored by Orientalists prove a strong presence of castle symbolism in Sufi literature. Aḥmad al-Ghazālī (d 520/1126) states, for exemple, that 'the heart, the spirit, and the most profound depths of the soul are linked unto a pearl which is within a shell which is within a cage within is within a room'.[12] Muḥyī al-Dīn ibn 'Arabī (d 638/1240) in his conception of the Night-Voyage to the Majesty of the Most Generous through the seven 'heavens' offers a paradigm of the seven rooms of the interior castle.[13]

8. Robert Ricard, 'Le symbolisme du 'Château intérieur' chez Sainte Thérèse', in *Bulletin Hispanique*, LXVII (1965): 25–41.
9. EW Trueman Dicken, 'The Imagery of the Interior Castle and its Implications', in *Ephemerides Carmeliticae*, XXI (1970): 198–218.
10. María M Carrión, 'Scent of a Mystic Woman: Teresa de Jesús and the Interior Castle', in *Medieval Encounters*, XV (2009): 130–56.
11. Miguel Asín Palacios, 'El símil de los castillos y moradas del alma en la mística Islamica y en Santa Teresa', in *al-Andalus*, 11 (1946): 267–268.
12. Aḥmad al-Ghazālī, *Kitab al-Tajrīd*, cited in Miguel Asín Palacios, 'El símil de los castillos y moradas del alma en la mística Islamica y en Santa Teresa', in *al-Andalus*, 11 (1946): 265–266.
13. Luce López-Baralt, *Islam in Spanish Literature: from the Middle Ages to the Present*, translated by Andrew Hurley (Leiden: Brill 1992), 119–120.

Lopez-Baralt dates the castle's metaphor to the origins of Islam. She cites a Muslim author of the ninth century for whom the castle is the metaphor of the inner life. Abū'l-Ḥusayn al-Nūrī (d 295/907), in Chapter VIII of his work *Maqāmāt al-Qulūb* (Stations of the Heart) describes the interior castle as having been created by God himself.[14]

Ankaravī, best known to specialists for his immense work of commentary on the *Mathnawī* of Rūmī,[15] is probably the most studied representative of the Ottoman Mevlevî tradition; his work on Rūmī was so appreciated in fact that a fifteen-volume translation into Persian of his comprehensive *Mathnawī* commentary was made in recent decades,[16] indicating that the genius of the Shaykh of Galata has not gone unnoticed elsewhere in the Muslim world. In the writings of Ankaravī and especially in his analysis of the rules and manners of dervish conduct which is the method of Mevlevî path, generations have learned the Mevlevî Sufi *adab*, mystical attitudes and religious customs. Understanding the mores of mystical courtesy or *adab* is crucial to understanding Sufi practices, to the comprehension of Islamic ethics in general, and finally, to grasping the personality of *homo islamicus*.[17] The whole life of the dervish adept is regulated on the basis of a code of ethical conduct and Sufi etiquette (*adab*)

---

14. Luce López-Baralt, 'Santa Teresa de Jesús y Oriente: el símbol de los siete castillos del alma', in *Revista sin Nombre* 12/4 (1983): 24-44; see also Luce López-Baralt, *Islam in Spanish Literature: From the Middle Ages to the Present*, translated by Andrew Hurley (Leiden: Brill, 1992), 91–142.
15. Alberto Fabio Ambrosio, 'Galata Mevlevihanesi'nde Şeyh Olmak (Being a Shaykh in Galata)', in *Saltanatın Dervişleri Dervişlerin Saltanatı İstanbul'da Mevlevilik/ The Dervishes of Sovereignty, the Sovereignty of Dervishes: the Mevlevi Order in Istanbul* (Istanbul: Araştırmalar Enstitüsü 2007), 42–56; Bilal Kuşpınar, *Ismā'īl Anqaravī on the Illuminative Philosophy: his* Īżāhu'l-Hikem: *its Edition and Analysis in Comparison with Dawwānī's* Shawākil al-hūr, *together with the translation of Suhrawardī's* Hayākil al-nūr (Kuala Lampur: International Institute of Islamic Thought and Civilisation 1996); Erhan Yetik, *İsmail-i Ankaravî. Hayatı, Eserleri ve Tasavvufî görüşleri* (Istanbul: İşaret 1992).
16. *Sharḥ-i kabīr-i Anqaravī bar Mathnawī-yi Mavlavī*, translated into Persian by 'Iṣmat Satārzāda (Tehran: Intishārāt-i Zarrīn 1374 A Hsh./1995), 15 volumes. See also Thierry Zarcone, 'Le *Mathnavî* de Rūmī au Turkestan oriental et au Xinjiang', in V Bouillier et Servan-C Schreiber (sous la direction), *De l'Arabie à l'Himalaya* (Paris: Maisonneuve et Larose 2004), 197–210.
17. Georges C Anawati, 'Homo Islamicus', in *Images of Man in Ancient and Medieval Thought: Studia Gerardo Verbeke ad amicis et collegis dicata*, in F Bossier *et al* (editors), (Louvain: Leuven University Press, 1976), 231–47.

that determines even his smallest gestures and behaviour. This code of conduct remains an essential element for any anthropological understanding of 'mystical' Islam.

Being one of the foremost representatives of the Mevlevî Sufi tradition of his day, Ankaravī in his handbook for the Sufis explains that the *dhikr/zikr* is itself a kind of *Samāʿ/semâ*.[18] Although in his *Minhâcü'l-Fukarâ*, which is a serious reference-point for determining the rites and doctrines of Mevlevî dervishes, Ankaravī writes sparingly on the metaphor of the castle, providing no little explanation or description of this castle—unlike other mystics who had used the symbol in both the Islamic and Christian (and Jewish) traditions—his definition suffices to suggest that his use of this metaphor was no accident. After quoting a *ḥadīth* that refers to the Muslim the profession of faith ('There is no God but God'), Ankaravī remarks, 'he who is within the circle of the profession of faith, is inside the Castle of God'. This *ḥadīth* reported by Ankaravī attests that 'He who says "there is no God but God" is protected within my castle, and he who is within my castle is safe from any anguish'.[19] It is clear that Ankaravī could very easily thus conclude that 'the word "castle" is used because the one who says that "There is no God but God", abandons all vanity and engages in worship of God'. The comparison is based on a metaphorical and an explicitly symbolic use of the image of the castle: the evil tendencies of human passion are abandoned outside of the castle; inside it the treasures represented by the profession of

18. Although the practice of repeating God's name is not mentioned in recent works as Rūmī's practice, it is well attested in the time of Ankaravî. Gölpınarlı (d 1982), the renowned Turkish scholar, argues that at the time of Mawlana, the practice and *adab* of *zikr* did not exist in the same form that would later be adopted by Ankaravī; consequently, the founder of the *ṭarīqat* could not have introduced what did not exist. Gölpınarlı, however, recognizes that through the testimony of the Shaykh of Galata in the seventeenth century the practice had obtained its recognition even among the Mevlevîs. Abdülbâki Gölpınarlı, *Mevlevî âdâb ve erkânı. Terimler, Semâ' ve Mukaabele, Evrâd ve tercemesi, Âdâb ve Erkân, Mevlevîlikte dereceler, Mesnevî okutmak, Metinler*, 1963 (Istanbul: İnkilâp 2006), 136–138.

19. İsmail Rusûhî Ankaravî, *Minhâcü'l-Fukarâ. Mevlevî Âdâb ve Erkânı Tasavvuf Istılahları*, edited by Safi Arpaguş (Istanbul: Vefa Yayınları 2008), 160. The *ḥadīth* in question is based on this version: 'God said by a holy *ḥadīth* that whoever utters the words: "There is no God but God" is in my castle. He who is in my castle is certainly safe from my punishment', which is cited in the *El-Sagir Câmiü* by Abū Abdu'llāh Muḥammad b Ḥasan b Al-Ferkad Ḥanifī Shaybanī (d 189/805).

faith are kept safe and secure. In essence, therefore, the profession of faith is the stronghold of God, and faith itself is then compared to the abode of God. One who remains preoccupied with the repetition of the name of God also dwells, metaphorically speaking, within the 'Castle of God'. Rather than the idea of being protected from evil, the image evokes the privacy and secrecy inherent in the practice of *dhikr/zikr*. Ultimately, therefore, those who practice the repetition of the great name of God, dwell in a castle, being sequestered within the sanctuary of the divine.

This same *hadith* can give rise to a new field of investigation on the prevalence of this symbol. In fact, it would seem that it goes back to the earliest centuries of Islam, even before Nūrī whose work López-Baralt has studied. Ankaravī, quoting the above *hadith*, highlights that the use of this symbol is deeply rooted in Islamic tradition. Another question would be to further investigate relations between Islamic symbols and their reflections and counterparts found in texts from other religious traditions.

In his interpretation, Ankaravī stresses that the Muslim profession of faith in the formula 'There is no god but God' is precisely the castle of God, the circle of divine unity (*daire-i tevhîde*). The circle, itself a symbol of divinity, is thus related to the profession of the unicity of God (*lâ ilâhe illallah*). The association between the two symbols is extremely meaningful. The circle and the castle are intimately linked. Both evoke the idea of divine unity. Thus those who dwell inside the divine space (circle and castle) are saved from any possible punishment, including divine. These few sentences would certainly have impressed themselves on the imagination of the disciple who read and studied Ankaravī's dervish handbook, where the importance of these spiritual symbols for training in the practice of the *zikr* would have been apparent.

Mevlevî *Zikr* and Mystical Unity

In hagiographic stories of Rumi, special attention is given to the practice of the repetition of the divine Name Allah. Aflākī, who was first among the biographers of the great mystic, thus posed the following question to Rūmī:

> What then is Khodāvandgār's way of performing the *dhekr* ? Mowlānā replied: 'Our dhekr-formula is Allāh, Allāh, Allāh (God! God! God!) because we are partisans of God (allāhiyyān). We come from God and unto God we shall return'.
> We are born of Essence and to Essence we travel.
> Companions, say blessings on behalf of our travelling.
> 'Indeed, having declared abandonment of everything but God, we have grasped onto God.'
> I have cleared away the two worlds from my side.
> Like the h I sit at the side of the l in Allah.[20]

According to what has been handed down to us from early biographers, Rūmī's conception of *zikr* was clearly focused on the name of Allah alone. In terms of Christian theology, we might even define Rūmī's doxology as favouring an exclusively theocentric language.[21] Indeed, according to the story related by Aflākī, one may deduce that Rumi wished to focus on the name Allah, even to the point of excluding all other formulas. Thus, one finds that this theocentric, Allah-focused attitude attributed to Rūmī becomes in subsequent periods even more emphasized by Mevlevî disciples in the doctrine, practice and culture of the *ṭarīqat*. One example will suffice. The pointed dervish hat or crown (Persian: *tāj;* Turkish: *taç*) that distinguished the members of the Sufi brotherhoods by the specific numbers of manifold corners or sides (Persian: *tark*), became for the Mevlevîs a round, unifold honey-coloured cone. Compared to other mystical Orders, the Mevlevîs are the only one in which this unifold headgear shaped like a cone with no folds appears, a design which takes its unique form from the monotheistic affirmation of the unity of God.

---

20. al-Aflâkî, *Şams al-Dîn Ahmed, Manâḳib al-'Arifîn (Metin)*, éd. Tahsin Yazıcı, (Ankara: Türk Tarih Kurumu Basımevi, 1976), volume 1, 250–51; Eflâkî, Ahmed, *Ariflerin Menkıbeleri*, trad. Tahsin Yazıcı, (Istanbul: Kabalcı 2006), volume I, 234; John O'Kane, *The Feats of the Knowers of God (Manâqeb al-'arefîn)* (Leiden: Brill 2002), 174.
21. Lloyd Ridgeon, 'Christianity as Portrayed by Jalāl al-Dīn Rūmī', in Lloyd Ridgeon (editor), *Muslim Interpretations of Christianity* (London: Curzon 2001), 99–126; Leonard Lewisohn, 'The Esoteric Christianity of Islam: Interiorisation of Christian Imagery in Medieval Persian Sufi Poetry', in Ridgeon (editor), 'Christianity as Portrayed by Jalāl al-Dīn Rūmī', 127–56.

In short, everything in Mevlevî spirituality seems to converge towards the proclamation of God's unity and the uncompromisingly absolute character of God's name.

Although the practice of remembrance of God in the heart (*dhikr* or *zikr)* is recorded in other sources from Rūmī's Order,[22] in the third chapter of his *Minhâc'ül-fukarâ*, Ankaravī describes the practise briefly, thanks to which—and to some of his other writings—the ritual of the Mevlevî *zikr* can be reconstructed. The text's intention was to describe and teach the ritual according to the example of the Mevlevî Order's founder. Here, the Shaykh of the Galata convent affirmed that Rūmī was always engaged in repetition of both the sublime divine Name (*ism-i celal*) and the simple third-person singular pronoun 'He' or 'Him' (*Hū*, which indicates, in this case, that 'He alone is God').[23] Ankaravī reaffirms the strong link between the *zikr* and the repetition of this Name of God, stating that during the *zikr* the Mevlevî Sufi sees nothing but the existence of God. The affirmation of the unity of God is the pinnacle of the practice of the *zikr*,[24] which for the dervish also means becoming free from everything ungodly (*mā-sawā'vAllāh*) through seeing all phenomena from the perspective of absolute Existence. Indeed, through the practice of *zikr*, the one who invokes (Perso-Arabic: *dhākir;* Turkish: *zakir*, that is, the one who practices *zikr*) becomes one with the One-Who-is-Remembered (Perso-Arabic: *madhkūr;* Turkish: *mezkûr*). As the Galatian master teaches his disciples, this practice must be conducted in the privacy of religious silence: '*Zikr* is not to make a racket and noise. Our *zikr* is with Him we remember; he who loses himself in Him Whose name is being remembered is the true practitioner. Being unaware of his own existence, he is already with God.'[25]

As can be noticed here, rather than pure technical description of the different practices of *zikr,* these few sentences are introduced by Ankaravī so as not to forfeit the deeper sense of the mystical technique in which the Mevlevî dervish was engaged and thus leave more room for spiritual values. His explanations of Sufi doctrine are interspersed with particular recommendations containing special details:

---

22. Safi Arpaguş, *Mevlevîlikte Ma'nevî Eğitim* (Istanbul: Vefa Yayınları 2009), 269–75.
23. Ankaravî, *Minhâcü'l-Fukarâ*, 165, 171.
24. Ankaravî, *Minhâcü'l-Fukarâ*, 162.
25. Ankaravî, *Minhâcü'l-Fukarâ*, 163.

> In this mystical Order, in the morning and in the evening, if they are in the *tekke* [Sufi meeting lodge] the dervishes are required to gather in a common place and to repeat aloud the sublime name together. Every novice must ask permission of his master (*halife*) who will inculcate the name to him, and whilst in solitude, the [Mevlevî] dervish will again repeat the name three thousand times. When he reaches the state of the *zikr* of the heart and the secrets of the *zikr*, then he can forget the external vocalization, because in that spiritual degree, the voice becomes the source of the *zikr*.[26]

Thus, the objective of the *zikr*'s practise is to achieve the silence in which the Sufi himself becomes, somehow, the source that continuously produces the sound of the sublime name of God. All day long, the Mevlevî dervish must interweave his daily chores with that name, even in the most profane moments: 'Every day, for example, around the table, after the meal and the ritual prayer, the dervishes intone *Hû*.'[27] Such absorption in the sublime name of God allows the Mevlevî to progress slowly but surely upon the Sufi path. As the Galatian master puts it, so many spiritual secrets are tied up in the act of repeating the sublime name of God that a thousand books could not contain all the different explanations.[28]

About a century later, Kösec Ahmad Dede (d 1777), who was affiliated with both the Nakşbendiye and the Halvetiye Orders, penned a treatise on the spiritual practices of the Mevlevîye of which he was also a member. In this work, Kösec explained the Mevlevî rituals in a much more detailed way. In his short chapter on *zikr*, he reaffirmed the attitudes formerly taught by Ankaravī. Kösec added that day and night, after the canonical prayers of dawn, afternoon, night and midnight, the Mevlevî dervish should repeat the name of God three thousand times, amounting to a daily total of twelve thousand repetitions.[29]

26. Ankaravî, *Minhâcü'l-Fukarâ*, 167.
27. Ankaravî, *Minhâcü'l-Fukarâ*, 169.
28. Ankaravî, *Minhâcü'l-Fukarâ*, 171.
29. Trabzonlu Köseç Ahmet Dede, *Et-Tuhfetü'l-behiyye fi't-Ṭarīqati'l-Mevlevîyye Tercümesi (Zâviye-i fukarâ). Mevlevîlik Âdâbı, Anektodlar*, edited by Ali Üremiş (Trabzon: Serander 2008), 22–23.

> For those who persist in invocation (*zakir*) of the vocal *zikr*, the *zikr* leads them to the heart. And as long as he does not reach the spirit (*ruh*) and the innermost secret core (*sır*), then he must continue to practice the *zikr* with the heart. In fact, the verbal vocalization strengthens the *zikr* of the heart, that of the heart strengthens that of the spirit, and finally the latter reaches the innermost secret core.[30]

Kösec Ahmed Dede adds that only when the *zikr* reaches the level of the spirit should the Mevlevî dervish be allowed to enter the *Samā*ʿ / *sema*; otherwise the dangers increase because 'in this case the *sema* instigates sensual pleasures, introduces the delights that are not of God and the unawareness of God increases'.[31] It is quite clear then that according to Mevlevî tradition itself, the *zikr* is inextricably associated with the *sema*. *Zikr* thus led to the *sema*, although it was not necessarily its only end.

It is interesting to read a similar linkage of *zikr* and *sema* in an account given by a great figure of nineteenth-century Ottoman Sufism, Aşçıdede Halil İbrahim (d 1906), who was himself a direct witness to this. Although İbrahim was personally connected by initiation to a branch of the Nakşbendiye-Halidiye and not officially affiliated to the Mevlevîye, he was a sympathizer (*muhibb*)[32] of the Order. In nearly two thousand pages of memoirs, he proves his attachment to Mevlevî spirituality. After recalling that among the Mevlevîye, the *zikr* is similar to that of Nakşbendî, he asserts:

> Without setting a tradition and without sticking to a particular time, it becomes a habit for the mystic to repeat the sublime name in silence and solitude, over the twenty-four hour period from midnight until midnight on the following day. During this period of time, at any moment, facing the direction of Mecca, maintaining a perfect attitude and devotion, after pronouncing the 'Bismillah', you can hear vocally the sound of the sublime name being repeated up to at least 66, 366 or 600 or even 1000 times, with the help of a counting instrument.[33]

---

30. Ahmet Dede, *Et-Tuhfetü'l-behiyye*, 22.
31. Ahmet Dede, *Et-Tuhfetü'l-behiyye*, 23.
32. Sezai Küçük, *Mevlevîliğin Son Yüzyılı*, 171.
33. Aşçı İbrahim Dede, *Aşçı Dede'nin hatıraları: çok yönlü bir sufinin gözüyle son dönem Osmanlı hayatı*, edited by Mustafa Koç e Eyyüp Tanrıverdi, volume II, (Istanbul: Kitabevi 2006), 1029.

Next follows the recitation of certain formulas of blessing regarded as classics in the Order, transcribed by the same author. Aşçıdede Dede, however, adds these very interesting details on how to practice the Mevlevî *zikr*, and perhaps, in his own way of telling it, we can observe the influence of Nakşbendiye doctrine in this statement:

> It should be understood here that during his invocation (*zikr*) of the sublime Name, the dervish pronounces the sublime word from the bottom of the right side of the chest to the left, back and forth, extending it during the movement between the two sides of his chest. He thus become preoccupied with *zikr* and the repetition [of the sublime name] that goes to and from like a telegraph line and its wires.[34]

This impressive description, illustrated with an image taken from modern technology such as the telegraph, confirms that *zikr* was still a living practice among the Mevlevîs at the end of the nineteenth century. Indeed, Aşçıdede Dede states: that:

> The invocation of the sublime Name of God is performed according to the customs of the Mevlevîye with the other dervish brothers on Monday and Friday nights after the final night prayers have been said, and again every morning after the morning ritual prayers.[35]

Likewise Aşçıdede Dede emphasizes the close relationship of *zikr* to *sema*, stating that, 'it is not a bad thing if the dervish, every time he beats the foot in silence and in secret during the practice of *sema*, also occupies himself with invocation of the sublime name of God'.[36]

While this testimony penned by Aşçıdede Dede in *fin de siecle* Istanbul is quite valuable, the descriptions of the Mevlevî *zikr* by Abdülbaki Gölpınarlı (d 1982) are even richer in terms of technical details. In 1963, the year of the publication of his book on Mevlevi rituals and manners (*Adab Mevlevî*), the Mevlevî tradition had become but a historical memory. For it to continue in some way and not to die out, the practice had to be recorded for posterity. It is for this reason that paradoxically speaking, it becomes easier to find

34. Aşçı İbrahim Dede, *Aşçı Dede'nin hatıraları*, 1029.
35. Aşçı İbrahim Dede, *Aşçı Dede'nin hatıraları*, 1029–1030.
36. Aşçı İbrahim Dede, *Aşçı Dede'nin hatıraları*, 1030.

technical descriptions of rituals such as the *sema* in documents of the twentieth century than in texts of previous centuries. In Gölpınarlı's reconstruction of the ceremony, the disciples are seated on the right and left of the Shaykh, forming a circle. The dervish in charge of preserving the Sufi circle's protocol (*meydancı dede*) first hands a rosary (*tesbih*) to the Shaykh, who then kisses it before handing it to the disciples, who pass it around to the other members of the circle. That is the reason for the big size of the *tesbih*, that can consist in even more than 1.000 beads. Everyone kisses the part of the rosary in his own hands. The Shaykh then intones the words 'I take in refuge in God from Satan the Accursed' (*Eûzü Billah Mine'ş-şeytani'r-Racim*)[37] in a solemn manner, followed by the beginning of Sura *Fātiḥa*: 'In the Name of the Most Compassionate, Most Merciful' (*Bismi'llāh al-raḥmān al-raḥīm*). Then he begins to chant three times the word 'Allah', prolonging the syllable 'Al' before pausing with a short stop during which he inhales briefly the second syllable 'lâh'. Without any interruption before the second syllable, 'Allāh' is then pronounced with a slight and indeterminate interval between the two syllables. By constant repetition, and by slightly lengthening the second syllable, the rhythm of the *zikr* speeds up. By reducing the interval between two syllables that are rather more pronounced, the *zikr* now gains more and more speed. When he says the first syllable, the leader makes a slight movement upward. At the second syllable, he returns to his natural position. It is not possible to rotate the head to the left and right. Continuing his *zikr*, the *tesbih* rolls towards the right, but without pulling hard the beads of the rosary. Towards the end, the sound of the letters softens so as to become almost inaudible. Only two sounds remain which are vocalised intensely. When the Shaykh considers the *zikr* ended, he utters 'Allāh' with a long-drawn-out exclamation and all remain seating bowing their heads in silence. Then follows the traditional invocation of the Order which concludes with an exhalation of the pronoun 'He' ('*Hû*' = God). The ritual now finally comes to an end and the Shaykh and his disciples, after uttering the usual salutations and litanies, rise to their feet. The Shaykh takes slow strides towards the centre of the room where he repeats the

37. Qur'ān, 12:98.

Mevlevî ritual salutation to all present. All go out, with a bowing of the head to the right and left.[38]

The precise times and places which are considered appropriate for the dervishes' collective invocation of the *Ism-i celal* are recorded by Gölpınarlı, who adds that any strange and unusual behaviour that may occur is not permitted and, indeed, the person who performs the rituals differently must quit the circle of the *zikr*. At very end of the *sema*, the *meydancı* approaches the Shaykh, leading another dervish with him, who then kneels and to whom this formula is recited: 'So know that He is One, there is no deity but Him: Allāh, Allāh', (*Fa'lem ennehû Lâ ilahe illallah; Allah, Allah, Allah*).[39]

Recent popular books published about the ritual merely repeat what these traditional authorities of the Mevlevî tradition—analyzed above—have passed on about this practice.[40] As we approach closer to the period when the Mevlevîye and their *Ṭarīqat* were outlawed by the Turkish secular state, one finds that the desire to record the fundamental practices of their Sufi spirituality becomes ever more insistent.

Conclusion: the Mevlevî Culture of Divine Unity

What seems most evident from our survey above of Mevlevî *zikr* and *sema* is the consistency of the Order and its rituals—all of which evoked a kind of culture of divine unity. Despite the aura of exoticism and heterodoxy conveyed by their famous *sema*,[41] the faith and culture propagated by the Mevlevîye was deeply rooted in the Muslim affirmation of the unity of God. Two points already mentioned above in this context should be reiterated here: the *sema* ceremony symbolic of the return to divine unity and the typical Mevlevî headgear (*sikke*) devoid of folds that indicates the simplicity of the one unit. Yet what of the hierarchical pyramid, less widespread in the universe of Sufi *Ṭarīqats*? The *çelebi*, the grand master of the Order, who lived in the

38. Abdülbâki Gölpınarlı, *Mevlevî âdâb ve erkânı. Terimler, Semâ' ve Mukaabele, Evrâd ve tercemesi, Âdâb ve Erkân, Mevlevîlikte dereceler, Mesnevî okutmak, Metinler*, 1963, (Istanbul İnkilâp 2006), 138–39.

39. Gölpınarlı, *Mevlevî âdâb ve erkânı. Terimler, Semâ'*, 139.

40. Hüseyin Top, *Mevlevî Usûl ve Âdâbı*, (Istanbul: Ötüken 2001), 167–72.

41. Bente Nikolaisen, 'Embedded in Motion: Sacred Travel among Mevlevi Dervishes', in S Coleman, & J Eade, *Reframing Pilgrimage: Cultures in Motion* (New York: Routledge 2004), 91–104.

tekke of Konya, was a direct descendant of Rūmī and represented the unity of the whole brotherhood.

Throughout its whole history, the essential Sufi discipline of *zikr* was the instrument of sublime glorification of the name of God (*ism-i celal*), for the Mevlevîye considered the name of Allāh, more than all the others, to proclaim the divine unity. The doctrine of simplicity had its source in the invocation of this divine name. As we have read, the accounts of the ritual of *zikr* and *sema* today handed down to us by Sufi mystics such as Ankaravī, Kösec Ahmad Dede and Aşçıdede Halil İbrahim, which enriched with the memory of the Order, were far from being dry records of instruction for the proper execution of the rite of *sema*. Indeed, the need to describe and to record the ritual grows only when challenged by its diminishing practice. As the authors point out, the Mevlevî adept must continually repeat the sublime name, everywhere, so as to become in a way—by adopting the divine character-traits and qualities—like the One they remember. While the practice of the invocation of the *Ism-i celal* merges with the *sema* ritual, it still remains an independent ceremony, both practices attesting to the mystic's encounter with the One.

In this regard, it is clear why the Mevlevî practices, despite the absence of an uninterrupted tradition, are today cherished by so many people, not only in Muslim countries, but throughout the world. The reason is that they have become a symbol for the fundamental belief of Islam, which is the profession of divine unity. Despite the simplicity of the rite, the Mevlevî *zikr* can produce an inner experience that occurs outside—an experience of the Sacred that may affect believer and unbeliever alike. The simplicity of the *sema* celebration of mystical unity goes hand in hand with the simplicity of its outward manifestation. The Mevlevî teacher Hüseyin Dede Azmi, writing in the late nineteenth century, could therefore assert:

> The issue of clapping the hands or invoking *Hayy* (God-the-Ever-living) or *Hū* makes complete sense, for if all these practices are part of religion, then the reason for their justification lies in the fact that the ecstasy they evoke [in both participants and onlookers] invades man independently of human will.[42]

42. Cited by Safi Arpaguş, *Mevlevîlikte Ma'nevî Eğitim* (Istanbul: Vefa Yayınları 2009), 275.

A Forum for Theology in the World Vol 6 No 2/2019

İsmā'īl Rusūhī Ankaravī: An Early Mevlevi Intervention into the Emerging Kadızadeli-Sufi Conflict

İsmā'īl Rusūhī Anḳaravī is one of the most important shaykhs who lived in Istanbul at the beginning of the seventeenth century. At the time, the Galata Mevlevīhāne where he lived and worked was one of the most influential Sufi sites in the Ottoman capital. On account of his location, which was close to both the European settlements and the Ottoman Court, this *tekke* was a place where the Mevlevī order could have an impact on both European and Muslim travellers alike.

This contribution aims to present the activities of this shaykh and his role in developing Sufi practice in the seventeenth century. His presence on the political scene discreet at best, and instead he sought, first and foremost, to give spiritual advice to the next generation of Mevlevī devotees.

Sufis and puritanical movements: a time of struggle

Anḳaravī lived in the midst of a struggle between various Sufi groups and the infamous movement of the *Ḳāżızādelīs*, who were agitating against religious practices they deemed to be deviations from proper Islamic belief and practice (*bid'a*).[1] This movement was marked by three periods of heightened activity against Sufi practices from the end of the sixteenth through the beginning of the seventeenth centuries. These three waves, marked by hostile preaching, were grounded in the thought of earlier Islamic scholar such as Ḳāżızāde Meḥmed, the

1. Madeline C Zilfi, *The Politics of Piety: The Ottoman Ulema in the Postclassical Age (1600–1800)* (Minneapolis: Bibliotheca Islamica, 1988); N Öztürk, *Islamic Orthodoxy among the Ottoman in the Seventeenth Century with Special Reference to the Qāḍī-Zade Movement* (PhD dissertation, Edinburgh University, 1981).

puritanical leader from whom the *Ḳāżızādelīs* drew their religious and political inspiration.

The stage was set by trials and executions of Sufis considered as marginal, heterodox or dangerous to the political and religious stability of the Ottoman Empire. During the early years of the career of one of the most important and respected jurisprudent of the Ottoman scholarly hierarchy, Ebussu'ūd Efendi (1490–1574), for instance, Oğlan Şeyh İsmā'īl Ma'şūḳī, a shaykh of the Bayrāmī-Melāmī order, was executed in 1529 along with twelve of his followers, based on the judgment of a group of jurisprudents that counted Ebussu'ūd among its members.[2] Another prominent Sufi leader, the sheikh Muhyī al-Dīn-i Ḳermānī in Istanbul, was executed in 1550 following a *decision issued by* Ebussu'ūd Efendi[3], followed by Shaykh Ḥamza' Bālī, was also decapitated in 1572–73. By this time, Ebussu'ūd had become the great *müfti* of the capital in 1545 by order of Sultan Süleymān[4], and his ruling increasingly challenged excesses that had come to mark some Sufi practices. This Muslim scholar thought that practices, such as Sufi *semā'* ceremonies[5] and various forms of movement that took place in them, which he defined as 'dancing' (*raḳṣ),* were prohibited

2. Reşat Öngören, 'Ebussuud'un Tasavvufi Yönü', in *Türk Kültürümüzde İz Bırakan İskilipli Âlimler (Sempozyum : 23-25 Mayıs 1997—İskilip)*, edited by Mevlüt Uyanık (Ankara: Türkiye Diyanet Vakıf Yayınları, 1998), 299.
3. Son of the Bayrāmī Shaykh Muhyī al-Dīn Yavsī (d 1514), Ebussu'ūd Efendi, became a prominent *Şeyh'ül-islām* and Hanafi scholar. He is frequently credited with legal and religious reforms aimed at re-organizing the Ottoman state during the time of Sultan Süleymān (1520-1566). He worked also to better integrate the Ottoman administrative system and Islamic religious law, forming the basis for the creation of the *Şeyh'ül-islām*'s position; see Pehlul Düzenli, 'Şeyhülislâm Ebussuûd Efendi: Bibliyografik Bir Değerlendirme', in *Türkiye Araştırmarları Literatür Dergisi* 3 (2005): 441–475; J Schacht, 'Abū l-Su'ūd', in *E. I,* I, 1960, 156; Colin Imber, *Ebu's-Su'ud: the Islamic legal tradition* (Edimbourg: Edinburgh University Press, 1997); J Schacht, 'Süleyman as Caliph of the Muslims: Ebû's-Su'ûd's Formulation of Ottoman Dynastic Ideology', in *Soliman le magnifique et son temps. Actes du Colloque de Paris. Galeries nationales du Grand Palais, 7-10 mars 1990*, edited by Gilles Veinstein (Paris: Ministère des Affaires étrangères, 1990), 179–184; Nihat Azamat, 'Ḥamza Bâlî', *DİA Diyanet İslâm Ansiklopedisi* (Istanbul: Türkiye Diyanet Vakfı İslâm Araştırmaları Merkezi, 1997), XV, 503–505.
4. Ahmet Yaşar Ocak, 'Idéologie officielle et réaction populaire: un aperçu général sur les mouvements et les courants socio-religieux à l'époque de Soliman le Magnifique', in *Soliman le magnifique et son temps* 185–192.
5. In the mevlevī tradition, the entire *semā'* ceremony is called *mukabele.*

by Islamic Law and must be banned. For this reason, he condemned in his *fatwas*, or formal religious opinions.[6]

A contemporary of Ebussu'ūd Efendi's was Birgivī Meḥmed Efendi, who received an Islamic education in the Ottoman schools, and is considered the true inspirator of the movement against sufis.[7] If Ebussu'ūd was, at the beginning of his career, in close proximity to the Bayrāmiye milieu, but left it subsequently, Birgivī maintained relations with a Bayrāmī shaykh throughout his life. This evidence suggests that his relation with Sufism was different, even though he stroke what he considered some invalid innovation in the field of the sufi practices too. As matter of fact, Birgivī had a very puritanical interpretation of the Islamic Law that lead him to fight everything was not according to it.

Birgivī instructed his followers by means of a very striking work: the *Ṭarīḳat-i Muḥammediye*.[8] Inspired by an approach similar to that of an earlier Muslim thinker and jurisprudent, Ibn Taymiyya (d 1328), the 'Muḥammadan Path' laid out by Birgivī is an invitation to the Muslim community to follow a path of virtuous commands. In another of his works, the *Maḳāmāt*, he also affirms that 'the Law is a tree, the *ṭarīḳa*, its branches; the divine knowledge (*ma'rifa*) its leaves, and the truth (*ḥaḳīḳa*) its fruits. If there is no tree, the others are not there either'.[9]

6. Ertuğrul M Düzdağ, *Şeyhülislâm Ebussuûd Efendi Fetvaları ışında 16. asır Türk hayatı* (Istanbul: Enedrun Kitabevi, 1983), 83–88; İsmail Safa Üstün, *Heresy and Legitimacy in the Ottoman Empire in the Sixteenth Century* (PhD diss, Manchester, 1991), 108–123.

7. Born in Balıkesir in 1522, Meḥmed Birgivī Efendi was educated in the religious sciences by Pīr 'Alī, his father. Afterward, he decided to join the Bayrāmī order. Later, the tutor of Sultan Selīm II asked to Mehmed Efendi to settle in Birgi, in order to preach in the new *madrasa* he had founded in this town; see Emrullah Yüksel, 'Birgivî', in *İA*, 6, 1992, 191–194; Ahmet Turan Arslan, *İmam Birgivî. Hayatı, Eserleri ve Arapça Tedrisatındaki Yeri* (Istanbul: Seha Neşriyat, 1992); Emrullah Yüksel, *Les idées religieuses et politiques de Mehmed Al-Birkéwî (929–981/1523–1573)* (PhD diss, Paris IV, 1972).

8. İmam-ı Birgivî Muhammed Efendi, *Tarikat-ı Muhammediyye Tercümesi*, translated by Celâl Yıldırım (Istanbul: Demir Kitabevi, 1996); Muhammed b. Pir Ali Birgivi, *Tarikat-ı Muhammediyye siret-i Ahmediyye*, edited by A Faruk Beşikçi (Istanbul: Kalem Yayınevi, 2006); Bernd Radkte, 'Birgiwī's Ṭarīqa Muhammadiyya. Einige Bemerkungen und Überlegunge', in *Journal of Turkish Studies*, 26/II (2002): 159–170.

9. Yüksel, 184–185.

Birgivī, like Ebussuʿūd, was an active participant in the struggle against Sufi practices, especially *semāʿ* and *raḳṣ*. At one point, he reminds his readers of a traditional interpretation of the earlier Muslim scholars, who argued that the Sufi practice of *semāʿ* and *raḳṣ* can be associated by analogy with agitated movements and frivolous play (*la'b*) and for this reason, they are forbidden by the religious law. The inclusion of *raḳṣ* is the first step toward libertine attitudes and it can pervert the otherwise laudable pronunciation of the name of God. The *fatwa* of Muḥammad al-Bazzazī (d 1424)—a prominent early Ottoman Hanafi jurist—cited on the authority of Ḳurṭubī is, in the eyes of Birgivī, evidence that *raḳṣ* was forbidden by the four Islamic law schools. The fact that he followed this fatwa and his treaty on the Path of Muḥammad set up the idea of an Hanbali orientation of Birgivī, even if this is not really the case.[10]

The movement that was inspired by Birgivī Meḥmed's treatise, *Ṭarīḳat-i Muḥammediye*, came to be picked up by a religious leader by the name of Ḳāżızāde Meḥmed (d 1635), from which the *Ḳāżızādelī* movement would take its name. Ḳāżızāde Meḥmed would be the figure who would be truly responsible for initiating a political, as well as religious challenge against Sufism in the Ottoman society. Naʿīmā, the great Ottoman historian, defined the events that followed as a division between the people of the Path and the followers of the *Ḳāżızādelī* agitation' *(Ehl-i ṭarīḳ ve tebaʿ-i Ḳāżızādeli fitreti)*.[11] The struggle that followed was marked by three major waves of activity.

The first wave was initiated by the aforementioned Şeyh Ḳāżızāde Meḥmed Ṭoğānī Muṣṭafā Efendi. Known as Ḳāżızāde Meḥmed[12], he was born in Balıkesir, probably in 1582. The fact that the father was a jurisprudent explains both his nickname and its use as term to define the entire movement he founded. Ḳāżızāde Meḥmed, after studying with his father, felt under the influence of the Birgivī's religious works.[13] In the capital, he also attached himself to the following of Ṭursunzāde 'Abd Allāh Efendi, who was considered as his *mu'īd*, or tutor. After completing his education, he began to practice as a preacher (*vāʿiz*)

10. Hüriye Martı, *Birgivî Mehmed Efendi. Hayatı, Eserleri ve Fikir Dünyası* (Ankara: Türkiye Diyanet Vakfı, 2008), 166–190.
11. Necdet Sakaoğlu, 'Kadızadeliler-Sivasîler', in *DBİA*, 4, (2003): 367–369.
12. Öztürk, 144.
13. Kâtib Chelebi, *The Balance of Truth*, translated by GL Lewis (Allen and Unwin Ltd, London, 1957), 132–134.

in different mosques of Istanbul. He was also attracted to the Sufi path after a meeting with the Halvetī shaykh of the Tercumān *tekke*[14], 'Ömer Efendi (d 1623), who became his spiritual guide for a time. But the mystical path was not to his liking, so he abandoned it and went back to being a preacher in the mosques of Murād Pāşā, Sultan Selīm, Fātiḥ and Beyazıt. In 1631, he assumed a position of some prominence as the preacher in the prestigious Aya Sofya mosque until his death in 1635 during the campaign of Revān.

In the first part of his treatise named *Risāle-i Ḳāżızāde,*[15] Ḳāżızāde Meḥmed attacked the legality of the practices of *semā'* and *raḳṣ*. Moreover, he also attacked a doctrinal opinion that had been issued a century before by a previous Ottoman şeyh'ül-islām, Zenbillī 'Alī Çelebi (d 1525). In the second part of his work, Ḳāżızāde focused on *bid'a*, or "unacceptable innovations/deviations", that represented what he viewed as the real problem facing the Ottoman Muslim community. The opposition to Ḳāżızāde Meḥmed was embodied by the Halvetī Sufi representative Şeyh 'Abd'ül-Mecīd Sivāsī Efendi (d 1639). Born in 1563 in Zile near Tokat, he rose to become a prominent shaykh of the Halvetī order.[16] Sivāsī studied the classical Islamic sciences with his uncle, Şems ed-Dīn Aḥmed Sivāsī (d 1597), who also became his spiritual guide Sivāsī, not only followed the path of his uncle but became his successor (*halīfe*) and represented the leadership of the Sivāsī branch of the order in Sivās. Sultan Meḥmed III (d 1603) called him back to Istanbul to act as the public preacher (*vā'iz)* at Aya Sofya; a post that would later be held by his rival, Ḳāżızāde Meḥmed. During this appointment, he was in charge of the *zāvīye* of Meḥmed Efendi built in 1585 in the Eyyüp neigbourhood; then as preacher he was sent firstly to Aya Sofya's, then to the Şehzāde's (in 1607), Sultan Selīm's (in 1609) and finally to that of Sultan Aḥmed's (since 1617) mosque, until his death in 1639. We can see in the Sivāsī's life two order of religious activities: the one as preacher and the other as shaykh.

14. M Baha Tanman, 'Dırağman Küllliyesi' in *DBİA*, 3 (1994): 49–51.

15. Mehmet Kadızade Efendi, *Risâle-i Kadızade*, in I. Doğmuş, *Türkiye'de XVII. Yüzyıldaki Dinî Çatışmalara Sosyolojik Bir Bakış (Kadızadeliler ve Sivasiler)* (Master Thesis, İzmir: Dokuz Eylül Üniversitesi, 2000), 134–137.

16. Cengiz Gündoğdu, *Bir Türk Mutasavvıfı Abdülmecîd Sivâsî (971/1563–1049/1639. Hayatı Eserleri ve Tasavvufî Görüşleri* (Ankara: TC Kültür Bakanlığı Yayınları, 2000), 3; Ekrem Işın, 'Abdülmecid Sivasî', in *DBİA*, 1 (1993): 52–53.

'Abd'ül-Mecīd Sivāsī is famous for his comments on the Mesnevī, the masterpiece of Mevlāna Celāleddīn Rūmī (d 1273), who was the inspirer of and founder of the Mevlevī order. Sivāsī's *Şerḥ-i Mesnevī* was a commentary on the verses of the *Mesnevī* up through the 1328th verse, and was grounded primarily in a Sufi perspective. For his efforts, Sivāsī earned the nickname of *Şāriḥ (The Commentator)*, because of his activity as commentator.

The religious debate between the two personalities was not just about the *semā'*, *devrān*, or whatever constituted *raḳṣ*, or 'dancing'. It also took up a more general range of issues tied to doctrine ideas and religious practices, such as and devotion to the Prophet, the faith of the Muḥammad's parents, the status of believer or not of the Faraon, the employ of melody of the Ḳu'rān and of some prayers's recitation, the cult of saints the consume of tobacco, coffee and some other stimulant drug, and some other counts.[17] If the *Ḳāżızādelī* preached that every *bid'a* was a potential danger for Muslim societies, on the other side, groups of Muslim scholars not aligned with the party of the *Ḳāżızādelī* upheld the legitimacy of the Sufi practices. The debate was thus open between two factions made up of Sufi and *Ḳāżızādelī* preachers that came to engulf also a wide range of Muslim scholars, and eventually, the Ottoman Court and the broader Ottoman population as a whole. Some of those in authority already feared the power of the various Sufi orders for their implicit character of independence from authority, because they became the symbols of the social reforms and, in accordance to this kind of indipendece from the official power, the synonym of degeneration.

This first step of the struggle was only an oral debate. In this situation, Anḳaravī takes part to the debate, with his own way of answer and offering a mevlevī interpretation. Two years after the death of the Galata's shyakh, Na'īmā relates that the night of 12 *Rabī'* I 1043/18 August 1633, both parties debated their positions in a hostile environment in the Sultan Aḥmed[18]. It was the beginning of the second step of the struggle and this event means that the first debate was not closed, and probably the answers of the Sufis were not enough

17. Kâtib Chelebi, *The Balance of Truth*, translated by GL Lewis (London: Allen and Unwin, 1957).
18. Madeline C Zilfi, 'The Kadizadelis: Discordant Revivalism in Seventeenth-Century Istanbul', in *Journal of Near Eastern Studies*, 45 (1986): 251–269.

The role of Anḳaravī in the beginning of religious disputes

Between the first and the second step of this struggle over the legitimacy of various Islamic practices, we can locate the activity of Anḳaravī. Born in Ankara at some point during the second half of the sixteenth century, we do not have at our disposal any significant references about his early life.[19] His full name, İsmā'īl Rusūhī Anḳaravī, suggests that he may have been affiliated with the Bayrāmiye at some point, and that he already had a good knowledge of Islamic sciences, because of his title (Rusūhī) that were done just to people with a good Islamic education.

When Anḳaravī was still living in Ankara, he got an eye sickness, most likely a cataract. In order to find a solution for his blindness, he decided to perform a pilgrimage to the tombstone of Mevlānā Rūmī (d 1273) in the hopes of saving his sight. This pilgrimage would prove to be an event that would influence all the future shaykhs of Galata. When he reached Konya, Anḳaravī met the successor of Rūmī and then-Master of the Mevleviye, Bostān Çelebi II (d 1705), who suggested he pray for recovery from his blindness. The new view corresponds to a kind of conversion to the Mevlevī Sufism. Anḳaravī's experience with the Mevlevī order in Konya, which resulted in the curing of his blindness, opened up a new spiritual period in his life. He entered into the Mevlevī order by pledging himself to Bostān Çelebi II. The few biographical records that survive about Anḳaravī say that he advanced quickly on the Mevlevī path and became an advanced mystical practitioner; so much so that he was appointed to the Galata Mevlevīhāne on the European side of the Ottoman capital of Istanbul. This *tekke*, also known as the *Ḳapıkule* (Monastery of the Servant's Tower), was built in 1492.[20] It needed a new guide, because

19. Erhan Yetik, *İsmail-i Ankaravî. Hayatı, Eserleri ve Tasavvufî görüşleri* (Istanbul: İşaret, 1992); Bilal Kuşpınar, *Ismā'īl Anqaravī on the Illuminative Philosophy, his* İżāhu'l-Hikem*: its Edition and Analysis in Comparion with Dawwānī's* Shawākil al-hūr, *together with the translation of Suhrawardī's* Hayākil al-nūr (Kuala Lampur: International Institute of Islamic Thought and Civilisation (ISTAC), 1996), 3–50; Semih Ceyhan, *İsmail Ankaravî ve Mesnevî Şerhi* (PhD diss, Uludağ Üniversitesi, 2005), 49-154.

20. Ismail Ünver, 'Galata Mevlevî-hânesi Şeyhleri', *Osmanlı Araştırmaları*, 14 (1994): 195–219; Can Kerametli, *Galata Mevlevihanesi. Divan Edebiyat Müzesi* (Istanbul: Türkiye Turing ve Otomobil Kurumu, 1977), 21; *The Garden of the Mosques. Hafız Hüseyin al-Ayvansarayî's Guide to the Muslim Monuments of Ottoman Istanbul*, trans. Howard Crane (Leiden/Boston/Köln: Brill, 2000), 368–373.

the former shaykh was sent to manage the *tekke* of Kasımpaşa. During Anḳaravī's lifetime, there were three Mevlevī *tekkes* in the Ottoman capital in addition to the Ḳapıkule: the Yenikapı Mevlevīhānesi[21] on the Marmara's seacoast that was founded in 1598; the Beşıktaş Mevlevīhāne which was opened in 1622;[22] and that of Kasımpaşa which was opened in 1623.[23] Anḳaravī arrived in Istanbul in 1610 and we don't know whether he came to Galata as a new shaykh appointed from outside the capital, or if he was appointed after spending a number of years in the city. He spent twenty-one years as the sheikh of the Galata Mevlevīhāne, along with his fellow shaykhs 'Abdī Dede (d 1631) in Kasımpaşa, Ağazāde Meḥmed Dede (d 1653) in Beşiktaş and Doğānī Aḥmed Dede (d 1630) in Yenikapı. The last of the four arrived at the Yenikapı Mevlevīhāne in the same year that Anḳaravī reached the capital, and he also worked to combat the movement of the *Ḳāżızādelī*.[24] This means that the Mevlevīs were a common front togheter the puritanical groups' interpretations. The year of Anḳaravī's death is recorded with different dates, but the most probable is 1631; he is buried in the Galata's Mevlevīhāne.[25]

Anḳaravī's life was devoted to the teaching of correct instruction for Mevlevī dervishes. His writings reflect this spiritual purpose; his commentary on the *Mathnawī* of Rūmī, the *Şarḥu'l-Mathnawī*, also known as the *Mecmū'at'l-Leṭā'if ve Meṭmūratu'l-Me'ārif*[26], proved to be a reference for all future commentaries, including that

21. Żīya Ḥāfıẓ Meḥmed 'Ārif Efendi Ḥafīdī Meḥmed, *Merākiz-i Mühimme-i Mevleviyeden Yeñi Ḳapū Mevlevīḥānesi* (Istanbul, 1329); Ihtifalci Mehmed Ziya Bey, *Yenikapı Mevlevihanesi*, translated by Murat A Karavelioğlu (Istanbul: Ataç Yayınarı, 2005); Crane, 253–254.

22. Crane, 420–423; M Baha Tanman, 'Beşiktaş Mevlevîhânesi', in *DİA*, 5 (1992): 553–554; Pars Tuğlacı, 'Çırağan Mevlevihanesi', in *Tarih ve Toplum*, 13 (1990): 364–365; Erdem Yücel, 'Beşiktaş (Bahariye) Mevlevîhanesi', *Sanat Tarihi Yıllığı* 12 (1982): 161–168; Erdem Yücel, 'Beşiktaş (Bahariye) Mevlevîhanesi', in *Türk Edebiyatı*, 45 (1977): 31-33.

23. Crowne, 337–338; M Baha Tanman, 'Kasımpaşa Mevlevîhânesi', in *DİA*, 24 (2001): 554–555; Erdem Yücel, 'Kasımpaşa Mevlevihanesi', in *Türk Dünyası Araştırmaları Dergisi* I (1979): 7–86.

24. Ziya Bey, İhtifalci Mehmed, 77–81.

25. Semih Ceyhan, *İsmail Ankaravî ve Mesnevî Şerhi* (PhD diss, Uludağ Üniversitesi, 2005), 148–151.

26. İsmā'īl Rusūhī Anḳaravī, *Mecmū'at'l-Leṭā'if ve Meṭmūratu'l-Me'ārif (Şerhu'l-Mesnevī)* (Istanbul: Matbaa-i 'Āmire, 1289/1872), volume 7.

of the early twentieth-century scholar Reynold Nicholson.[27] Based on a combination of Qur'anic interpretations and Sufi traditions, Anḳaravī tried to link Rūmī's spiritual and poetic sensibilities with the theoretical approach of Ibn al-'Arabī's mysticism. He also has a preference for linguistic commentary—probably because of his knowledge of both Arabic and Persian—and he very often starts by addressing etymological issues. This fact could confirm what some scholars think of the commentary of Anḳaravī; overly linguistic in orientation. Yet from another point of view, given the context he was working in, Anḳaravī was forced to focus on the linguistic elements in his commentary. In order to defend the Sufi path, making a proper definition for his audience on the meaning of words whose origin was Arabic or Persian was very much needed by his Turkish-speaking audience. Some problems in regard to some Sufi practices, for example, had an etymological origin, such as *semā* and *raḳṣ*, which the *Ḳāżızādelī* tried to paint as innovation (*bid'a*).

Anḳaravī commented on the six volumes (*defter*) that comprised the masterpiece of Rūmī, the Mesnevī. The seventh volume, however, was an apocryphal one that appeared during Anḳaravī's lifetime, and whose authenticity was considered suspect and heavily debated. Regarding Anḳaravī's other commentaries, some of them concern Qur'anic suras[28], and others deal with prophetic tradition[29] and classic works of Sufism such as those of Şihab al-Dīn Suhrawardī (d 1191), Ibn al-Fāriż (d 1235) and Ibn al-'Arabī (d 1240).

Among the treatises that aim to defend the Mevlevī *semā*',[30] the best-known is the *Risāletü'l-ḥüccetü's-semā*',[31] because it was associated

27. Reynold Alleyn Nicholson, *The Mathnawí of Jalálu'ddí Rúmí*, volume 8, edited by RA Nicholson (London: Luzac & Co, 1925–1937).

28. İsmā'īl Rusūhī Anḳaravī, *Fātiḥa-ı tesfīr-i futūḥāt 'ayniye* (Istanbul: Matba'a-i Aḥmed Kāmil, 1328/1910).

29. İsmail Ankaravî, *Hadislerle Tasavvuf ve Mevlevî Erkânı, Mesnevî Beyitleriyle Kırk Hadis Şerhi, (Şerh-i Ahâdîs-i Erbaîn)*, ed. Semih Ceyhan (Istanbul: Dârulhadis, 2001).

30. İsmā'īl Rusūhī Anḳaravī, *Er-Risāletu't-Tenzīhiye fī şe'nī'l-Mevleviye* (Süleymaniye Kütüphanesi, MS Nafız Paşa 365); Ahmed Nezih Galitekin, 'İsmail Rusûhî Ankaravî ve Risale-i Muhtasara-i Müfide-i Usûl-i Tahîkat-i Nâzenîn', in *Yedi İklim* 8 (1994): 92–95.

31. İsmā'īl Rusūhī Anḳaravī, *Risāletü'l-ḥüccetü's-semā'* (Cairo: Bulaq, 1256/1840); İsmail Ankaravî, *Minhacu'l-Fukara*, ed. Saadettin Ekici (Istanbul: İnsan Yayınları, 1996), 365–393.

with another important Anḳaravī work, the *Minḥāc'ül-fuḳarā'*[32] where he gives a full synopsis of his teaching for the Sufi novice. In the latter work, which was divided into three parts with ten chapters each, Anḳaravī tried to explain the bases and the secrets of the Mevleviye. However, since the *Minḥāc'ül-fuḳarā'* was not designed to be an apologetic treatise, he referred to his epistle on the subject instead. This is the reason why both have been printed together from the nineteenth century up until the present.

Anḳaravī's last work is a selection of materials chosen from the *Mesnevī* and called the *Nisāb'ul-mevlevī*.[33] In this work, Anḳaravī explains the foundations of Mevlevī life by drawing on expressions found in Rūmī's work. He likewise used the same approach when he wrote a commentary of forty hadiths choosed by the different traditions; he used them as a foundation by which he could discuss Mevlevī practices in the light of the Prophetic *Sunna*.

After a lifetime of producing intense educational works, he died in the same *tekke* where he began his life of spiritual service. His importance to the Mevlevī order was recognized a century and a half later by Shaykh Ġālib, a late eighteenth-century Mevlevī leader and inspiration for a reform movement in the Ottoman poetry, who dedicated some verses to Anḳaravī as the Great Commentator on Rūmī's masterpiece:

> O Gālib! Here is the Master of the Masters in the path of Mevlānā
> He is the Excellent Commentator, Rusūhī,
> an exemplar for the people of Rusūh.[34]

As a Mevlevī shaykh, İsmail Anḳaravī taught his disciples about the Mevlevī Path, especially in creating a symbolic universe. The spiritual goal behind the *Minḥāc'ül-fuḳarā'* was to present the secrets of the

32. İsmā'īl Rusūhī Anḳaravī, *Minḥāc'ül-fuḳarā'* (Cairo: Bulaq, 1256/1840); İsmail Ankaravî, *Minhacu'l-Fukara*, edited by Saadettin Ekici (Istanbul: İnsan Yayınları, 1996).

33. İsmail Ankaravî, *Nisâbü'l Mevlevî (Tasavvufî Konulara Göre Mesnevî'den Seçmeleri)*, edited by Yakup Şafak and İbrahim Kunt (Konya: Tekin Kitabevi, 2005).

34. The word 'rusūh' here refers to people who as good knowledge in the field of the Islamic sciences and probably in a sufi perspective. Kuşpınar, 16; Server Dayıoğlu, *Galata Mevlevihanesi* (Ankara: Yeni Avrasya Yayınları, 2003), 147–151.

Mevlevī Path, the law—in terms of the Mevlevī five pillars of the religion—and the path to understanding the divine unity. The Mevlevī path was presented in a pious and faithfully Muslim way,[35] but the mystical perspective proposed by Anḳaravī is even more important.

According to the *Minḥāc'ül-fuḳarā'*, the Mevlevī path is composed of three spiritual circles: Mevlevī practices (the first section of the work); basic religious obligations (the second section); and the initiation' step to the divine unity (the third section)[36]. These sections are not organically separate from each other; rather, they represent three possible interpretations that overlap and intersect with each other. Anḳaravī's methodology in doing this is clear: whoever really desires to enter onto the Mevlevī path could not forget the basic pillars of Islamic doctrine and praxis. Still, this is only one aspect of the journey, for at the same time, the adepts should keep in mind that they are forming a union with oneness. A Mevlevī adept's education starts with their formal entrance into the Mevlevi order, but this should be done purely for spiritual purposes. Anḳaravī is especially critical of those who seek to join the order as a means of securing access to a daily meal rather than pursuing their spiritual goals. This demonstrates that a careful examination of this otherwise introductory work can yield very interesting insights: Anḳaravī inadvertently gives a vivid description of how many of his fellow Ottoman subjects approached religion at the time, and indicates that the motives that pushed people to join the Mevlevī Path were not always pure. For these reasons, all his teachings in the book strongly push the Mevlevī adept toward disciplining his will and his attitudes, both external and internal.

The first part of the Minhac commences with a discussion of the meaning of the spiritual guide, or *halīfe*. It is a kind of doctrinal and, in another sense, theological meditation on the role of the deputy of God, the Prophet. According to Anḳaravī, remaining true to the historical tradition of Sufism, the role of the *halīfe* is fundamental in any of his followers' education. That is why the spiritual guide must be a perfected guide; as Anḳaravī puts it, 'the *halife* is not a sinner, but someone who conforms his decisions and his pious activities to God's mysteries. He must let his heart become open to God's will, because

35. Anḳaravī (Cairo: Bulaq, 1256/1840), 26.
36. *Merātib-i sülūkü ve derecāt-ı Mie'yi.*

he represents an intermediary between God and his people.'[37] This sentence also indicates why a shaykh can ask for anything from his followers, and they must be as the corpse in the hands of the washers before a funeral.

This does not mean, however, that the follower is exempt from having some virtues and developing an orientation toward obedience and submission to God's will. A relationship that flows between the master and the disciple is also essential for Sufism's doctrine and practice. The *mürīd*, being the one who bends his will toward obeying his guide, must be motivated to perform all the practices of the order and to follow its customs. The goal is to reach a state of Union with God, but this final goal can only bereached by passing through various stages that involve a training of willpower, attitudes and human and natural behaviors. The life in a *tekke*, traveling from one Sufi place to another in the quest for the Truth, development of spiritual friendships through conversation (*soḥbet*) and all Mevlevī practices in general are aimed at education and training to prepare for obtaining the mystical state of union. As Anḳaravī says, 'the highest degree in the Path is a place conquered after many efforts, passing through all stages with love and passion. At this level, everything occurs at the same time: sadness, anguish, pleasure, goodness, badness, praise, shame, blessing, grace, blame and reproach.'[38]

The most well known practice of the Mevlevī order, celebrated in particular by Western travellers and observers as the dance of the whirling dervishes, is the *semā'*. Anḳaravī concludes the first part of his discussion in the Minhac by teaching his readers about it. This is evidence that for him, the synthesis of all the Mevlevīs' practices was embodied in the whirling dance, and that he interpreted it as a fulfilment of the whole Sufi experience. Many travellers defined this strange custom more than a simple dance[39], but a special ceremony or a kind of cosmic dance and Anḳaravī did not reject this interpretation. However, he mixed this idea with some other approaches as well. Ibn al-'Arabī's works are, in this perspective, fundamental for thinking about and outlining the foundations of the Mevlevī *semā'*, even if Ibn 'Arabī and Rūmī were not, in the twelth century, belonging

37. Anḳaravī (Cairo: Bulaq, 1256/1840), 21.
38. Anḳaravī (Cairo: Bulaq, 1256/1840, 26.
39. Reinhold, Schiffer, *Oriental panorama: British travellers in 19th century Turkey*,(Amsterdam: Rodopi, 1999), 200–204.

to the same mystical tradition. If Rūmī were more oriented to a metaphorical and poetical mysticism, Ibn 'Arabī tried to settle the basis of a mysticism's theory. From this perspective, a geometric and symbolic interpretation of the movements that made up the Mevlevī *semā'* constitutes the basis for the imaginary world. The symbolic geometry of the Mevlevī movements strike the human imagination and inspire its spirituality, and Anḳaravī even goes on to explain the categories of believers in term of geometrical curves:

One of the more subtle symbols of whirling (*devr*) is represented by the fact that the Mevleviye initiation (*sülūk*) is more circular, that is evident when the dervishes are whirling, and they are not like those of the linear way (*mustaṭīl*). In fact, the seekers (*ṭālibān*) of the truth can be divided into two categories. The first one consists of those who, from puberty until death, follow the Islamic Law (*şarī'at*) and the path of the order (*ṭarīḳa*). But some levels they can achieve, *cismānī* (bodily) or *ruḥānī* (spiritual), they believe that the truth is somewhere else and they separate it (*tenzīh*) [from any attribution]. They assume that it is neither in the highest level, or that it lacks a level of progression (*bilā mertebe*). They seek it for a very long time and with long talk (*diraz*). Those who have this opinion (*i'tiḳād*) possess the linear path (*mustaṭīl*). The other category includes those to whom, beginning the initiation (*ṭarīḳ-i sülūk*) with the help (*himmet*) of their spiritual master and the belief in God (*Ḥaḳḳ 'ināyeti*), have revealed for them (*münkeşif*) the oneness of existence (*vaḥdet-i vücūd*). In any level they have attained, they find the secret of the verse, 'wherever you turn, there is the face of God'.[40] And wherever they are, they see the manifestation of God (*Ḥaḳḳ müntecelli*) in everything. They are called 'those of the circular path' (*ṭarīḳ-i devriye ṣāḥibī*). Their travel is from the Truth (*min al-Ḥaḳḳ*), to the Truth (*ilā al-Ḥaḳḳ*) with the Truth (*ma' al-Ḥaḳḳ*) and in the Truth (*fī al-Ḥaḳḳ*). So, they find the true circularity.[41]

Thus, for Anḳaravī, the 'circular way' is not just a representation of the whirling dance, it is more of a philosophy to be employing before engaging in any kind of Sufi ritual. Or, in other words, the Sufi, and especially the Mevlevī *semā'* is circular because the envisioned journey toward approaching God has a circular shape. Anḳaravī, perhaps

40. Ḳur'ān II, 215.
41. Anḳaravī (Cairo: Bulaq, 1256/1840), 74.

drawing on some Islamic traditions that preceded him, thought that the existence, or even the image of the One had a circular shape. In the Arabic mathematical tradition, there are some treatises that try to show that the point and the circumference are the most perfect figures over all others. Moreover, even the direction of the canonical Islamic prayers is a kind of a big circle around the world's center, as represented by the Ka'ba in Mecca. This geometric representation then, has a strong impact on the dervish by reinforcing this circular image by various means upon his consciousness.

Anḳaravī also asserted that:

> this existence is a circular one (*bu vücūt vücūt-u devriye*). That is the reason why, for example, we can make the hypothesis that the essence of Oneness (*ẕāt-ı eḥādiyet*) is like a point from whom, before the [creation of the] world and humanity, comes a line (*haṭ*) tracing a circle (*dā'ire*) . . . like the line of the circle, the right side from the point represents the outer world (*ẓuhūr*), while the left side tells the inner one (*baṭūn*), and when both meet each other there is what we call the position of mankind (*mertebe-i insān*). Afterwards, the world and mankind come to the existence as a manifestation of the point of the essence, and they walk around the circle of existence.[42]

For Anḳaravī, then, the *semā'* is a way to relive the history of mankind and a good way to conceive of the progress of returning to its point of origin. He is perfectly aware that his explanation is just an introduction, complex though it may be, to the mystical universe. He can conclude his reflections about Mevlevī ritual by writing that:

> God Almighty revealed to this poor man[43] many other things besides the symbols, words and mysteries that were talked about here. His detailed topic is not the present synthesis, otherwise it would require another entire book. Intelligent men (*'āḳıl*) need just a sign that the meaning (*maḳṣūd*) rises from the horizons. God is the One who knows better.[44]

42. Anḳaravī (Cairo: Bulaq, 1256/1840), 70; Ekici, 265.
43. Anḳaravī, like most Ottoman writers, refers to himself through the use of a dismissive third-person construction.
44. Anḳaravī (Cairo: Bulaq, 1256/1840), 75–76.

This sentence indicates that the Mevlevī *semā'* is not a mere practice, but lies at the heart of Anḳaravī's work. The fact that the section on the Mevlevī *semā'* falls in the middle of the *Minhācü'l-fuḳarā'* is a sign of its importance in the order's mystical initiation. It is located exactly at the end of the second section of the work, before the beginning of the third section which is devoted entirely to the mystical ladder composed of one hundred spiritual steps. Therefore, the end of the Mevlevī ritual of the *semā'* marks the foundation for the inner mystical journey. In other words, it is a new beginning in itself, not an end point.

The geometric representation of the *semā'*: the point of contestation

The heart of the Mevlevī's order as expressed in the *Minhāc*, in a philosophical sense, is also central to the struggle against sufi practices. The reasons for the clash over Sufi rituals center on the explanations, interpretations and symbolic representations of them. If the Kadızādeli preachers were so convinced of the illegality of the *semā'*, and if they worked towards its prohibition, the Qur'an and Sunna were their first sources for their argument, which was a normal and necessary part of Islamic doctrine. But the choice to attack Sufism by way of its practices was not without consequences. Why was the *semā'*—among some others—a point of contestation? The *ẕikr*, or remembrance of God, was another target in which the preachers sought to find doctrinal elements that allowed for its condemnation. If the *ẕikr* could be attacked, *semā'* was even more vulnerable, as the latter built on the foundation of the former. Doctrinal disputes on Sufi practices thus became the major point of argument for the two factions, as opposed to abstract theological doctrines. Those who backed the *Ḳāżızādelīs* position held that the *semā'* was not permitted because of its closeness to the frivolous activities. The physical activity of what the *Ḳāżızādelīs* deemed to be dance, or *raḳṣ*, was too much ambiguous to allow for complete acceptance. Anḳaravī repeatedly states in his works that the *sema* is not a kind of game or amusement.[45]

In one of his explanations of Mevlevī practices, done in the form of a commentary on forty separate hadiths of the Prophet Muḥammad,

45. Anḳaravī (Istanbul: Dârulhadis, 2001), 56–59.

Anḳaravī reminded his readers that Rūmī talked about the *semā*ʿ in only two parts of the *Mesnevī*. This remark is linked to a subsequent point where he states that Sultan Veled, Rūmī's son and the real founder or the Mevleviye, confirms, in his *Ibtidā*ʾ*-nāme*, that Rūmī did experience mystical and spiritual states (*vecd ve ḥāl*) and dance and mystical movements (*raḳṣ ve ḥareketler*). Anḳaravī who supports the sure opinion of Sultan Veled, refers also that idea of those who supported that Rūmī didn't perform any sufi dance (*raḳṣ, ḥareket ve semā*ʿ *yapmadı*).[46] Again, when looking at this statement of Anḳaravī's, one senses the fearful sermons of the *Ḳāżızādelīs* preachers that were stoking the imagination of many, even among the Sufis themselves. The strategy of this movement was not only to reject the legality of Sufi rituals, but even sought to rewrite the historical record of the great saints' practices and, in this case, to cancel the idea that Rūmī performed these practices. The answers of the sheikh İsmāʿīl to these detractors, is in order to support the Mevlevī tradition with the witness of great saints.

Anḳaravī tried to avoid getting too involved with the conflict that would deteriorate into Ḳāżızādelī repression by the second half of the seventeenth century. He mentioned an opponent of the Mevlevī order in only one of his treatises, a shaykh named İbrāḥīm who had criticized the *semā*ʿ. In this case, Anḳaravī issued a response in Arabic to this shaykh; however, this was an exception. He otherwise did not take up a hostile position against other people in his society. He could not know the consequences that would arise out of the growing friction between the Sufis and their detractors, so he engaged himself in writing introductions to Mevlevī thought and practice instead. Thus, he did not engage so much in apologetic as in offering symbolic and doctrinal explanations to the uniniated about how Mevlevī ritual worked.[47]

Even when he did write treatises to defend Mevlevī praxis, the tone of his writings was more oriented towards finding good reasons

46. Anḳaravī (Istanbul: Dârulhadis, 2001), 59.

47. Alberto Fabio Ambrosio, 'Ecrire le corps dansant au XVIIe siècle : Ismâʿîl Rusûkhî Anqaravî', in *Le corps et le sacré en Orient musulman*, edited by Catherine Mayeur-Jaouen and Bernard Heyberger (Aix-en-Provence: Editions Edisud, 2006), 195–209; Alberto Fabio Ambrosio, 'La danse des 'derviches tourneurs' et la création d'un espace sacré', in *Journal of the History of Sufism*, 4 (2003/2004): 97–105.

to perform the *semā‘*. From the Sufi viewpoint, the point is not just fidelity to the Qur'an, but to understand a secret meaning of the Holy Book. Anḳaravī refers, in the titles of some of his manual's chapters, to what he called 'the secrets'. The secrets represent a the symbolic explanation of various Mevlevī practices, and in particular the *semā‘*. The aforementioned symbolic and geometric interpretation was, for Anḳaravī and his contemporaries, a way to bypass the hindrances caused by the *Ḳāżızādelīs* preachers' position. The symbolic and geometric interpretations let Anḳaravī act as a representative of a mystical order, and moreover, as a point of linkage between the Tradition (Sunna) and the Sufi tradition as laid out in the Mevlevī order's initiation rites.

In the end, this kind of interpretation, based on symbolic analysis and a geometric perspective, involved the perception of believers toward their society. First of all, the position of the Sufi in the *semā‘* is not an isolated one. The Sufis, face to face at the beginning of the celebration of the *semā‘* (*muḳābele*), serves as a reminder of a Prophetic Tradition: 'the believer is the mirror for a believer'. This orientation, face to face, expresses a Muslim doctrine as expressed by the Tradition. Moreover, the canonical prayers of Muslims five times a day serve a similar purpose in this model. The Ka'ba is the center of all Muslim prayers, and at the moment all believers pray, they realize the circumference of the world around the Ka'ba in a similar visual representation to that of the *semā‘*.[48] In this sense, the form and function of the Mevlevīs in their *semā‘* is perfectly legitimate according to the symbols of Islamic doctrine. From an anthropological point of view, this Mevlevī practice of standing face to face in the *muḳābele* was fundamental in order to create a new interior image and a new status for the believer. The preachers rejected probably this spiritual position, quite different from the one of the canonical prayer. This new vision of the believer, for the Mevlevīs, was based on the fact that the form and function of their practices and rituals created a universe parallel that of the Islamic legal edifice of the classical period. The Mevlevī order, like others, was an element of Ottoman society and the fact that dervishes can be pointed out simply by their customs, their clothes and mostly by their *tekke*, could constitue a political hindrance

48. Attilio Petruccioli, *Dar Al Islam. Architecture du territoire dans les pays islamiques* (Wavre: éditions mardaga, 1995), 33–40.

for the unity of the society, by the different religious practice.[49] While not new in Islamic history, at that time in the Ottoman Empire, the growing differences in religious field did not just remain in the sphere of religious discussion anymore, they had been become the 'politics of piety' as Madeleine Zilfi called them.

The Sufis existed as a part of the community and the existence of different forms of religious society challenged any attempt to construct unity in an Ottoman Islamic society. The earlier periods of Ottoman history were marked by the existence of religious difference, in contrast to later periods where trends and religious currents became increasingly fixed and constrained. In his own time, Anḳaravī tried to maintain the equilibrium between the different religious currents, recognizing the essential place of Muslim traditions and foundations, but also seeking to carve out a place for that of the Sufis as well.

After Anḳaravī: the struggle for the victory

After Anḳaravī's time, a new stage of the escalation between Sufi and *Ḳāżızādelīs* partisans appears in the Ottomans religious history. Üsṭüvānī Meḥmed Efendi as a descendant of Ḳāżızāde Meḥmed's party and 'Abd'ül-Eḥad Nūrī, the defender of the Sufi position are the personalities of the second step of the debate. Üsṭüvānī Meḥmed Efendi (d 1661),[50] after an Islamic education in Damascus and Cairo, rose to the position of public preacher in the capital, particularly in several different religious centers such as the Semākī, Sultan Aḥmed

49. M Baha Tanman, 'Ottoman Architecture and the Sufi Orders: Dervish Lodges', in *Sufism and sufis in ottoman society. Sources-doctrine-rituals-turuq-architecture literature and fine arts-modernism*, edited by Ahmet Yaşar Ocak (Ankara: Publications of the Turkish Historical Society, 2005), 317–381; Maurice Cerasi, *La citta del levante : civilta urbana e architettura sotto gli Ottomani nei secoli XVIII-XIX* (Milano: Jaca Book, 1986), 252–258.

50. Üsṭüvānī Meḥmed Efendi was born in Damascus in 1608. After receiving an education in the Umayyad Mosque, he spent several years in Cairo before coming back by boat. During his journey he was captured by the French, who subsequently released him. In Istanbul, he switched to the Hanafī law school, giving up his ancient orientations through the Ḥanbalī and Shafi'ī Law traditions. Üsṭüvānī did not appear to leave any writings; we have only records of his oral teachings in the form of the *Kitāb-ı Üsṭüvānī* or *Üsṭüvānī risālesi*. Despite, the sultan's favor on him, his provocative sermons in Fātih Mosque was to incitate the violence against Sufis, was one of the reasons for the exile of Üsṭüvānī in 1656 to Damascus, where he died in 1661. Öztürk, 220–226.

mosques and Fātiḥ Mosque where he gained a multitude of followers. Interestingly, some of these followers were powerful members of the tradesmen (*esnāf*) very near to the Ottoman Court.[51] In 1651, a rebellion of the guilds was noted by the historical sources because of newly-introduced tax laws on the part of the Sultan. The alliance between the guilds and the *Ḳāżızādelīs* movement became increasingly evident from this point forward. The aversion to any innovation was a principle shared among the members of these influential groups, which dovetailed with that of the *Ḳāżızādelīs* preachers.[52] From this perspective, we can observe that in order to defeat the influential Sufi groups in the Ottoman context, the *Ḳāżızādelīs* began to realize that they were going to need allies beyond the Ottoman power. What served the political interests of the corporation just happened to also intersect with the conservative principles in religion espoused by the *Ḳāżızādelīs* movement.

In any case, Üsṭüvānī gained direct access to the Ottoman elites, especially he was under the protection of Reyḥān Ağa, the tutor of the Sultan, given that he was called the 'Pādişāh's *şeyh*'.[53]

In 1650, during the government of the grand vizier Melek Aḥmed Pāşā (d 1662),[54] the puritanical party obtained from some Ottoman officials an order to destroy several Sufi convents (*tekkes*). They succeeded in destroying the Halvetī *tekke* of Demir Ḳapı and in attacking a number of Sufis. When they began to attack the *tekke* at Atmeydanı[55], one of the Janissary corps, 'Ömer Ağa (d 1652), a follower of the halvetī shaykh 'Ömer Efendi (d 1658) sent some soldiers to defend the place, and he went himself, on the evening, to perform a *ẕikr* in order to stop them and to show their force. The second-in-command of the Janissary corps, the *Ḳul Kethüdāsı*, who admired 'Ömer Efendi, intervened to obtain from the Grand Vizier

51. Anton Minkov, *Conversion to Islam in the Balkans. Kisve Bahası Petitions and Ottoman Social Life, 1670–1730* (Leiden/Boston: Brill, 2004), 113–125 and 128–129.

52. Eunjeong Yi, *Guild Dynamics in Seventeenth-Century Istanbul. Fluidity and Leverage* (Leiden/Boston: Brill, 2003), 213–242.

53. Mehmet Kadızade Efendi, 87–127.

54. Fikret Sarıcaoğlu, 'Melek Ahmed Paşa', in *DİA*, 2 (2004): 42–44; Robert Dankoff, *The Intimate Life of an Ottoman Statesman Melek Ahmed Pasha (1588–1662): As Portrayed in Evliya Çelebi's Book of Travels (Seyahatname)* (Albany: State University of New York Press, 1991).

55. M Baha Tanman, 'Sofular tekkesi', in *DBİA*, 7 (1994): 24–25.

another ferman that would be against the puritanical party members, but the Kadızadelis responded by trying to have a fatwa declared by the şeyh'ül-islām Bahā'ī Efendi (d 1654)[56] that would establish the illegal character of the *devrān* and *sema'*. However, the *Ḳāżızādelīs* seem to have overplayed their hand, because they framed their letter against the Sufis in such violent language that the şeyh'ül-islām balked and refused to deliver the legal verdict that they wanted. In fact, he proved more favorable to the Sufi orders, especially the Mevleviye and the Halvetiye. Üsṭüvānī then tried to refer his complaints directly to the Grand Vizier and to the Shaykh al-Islām, by the mediation of the *Reīsü'l-küttāp*, but the official recognized the dangers of the possible clashes that could ensue, so he forbade all *Ḳāżızādelīs* from speaking out against the Sufis.

Some years after the death of 'Abd'ül-Eḥad Nūrī Efendi (d 1651),[57] the Üsṭüvānī's opponent and the shaykh of the Meḥmed Ağa *tekke* and also preacher in different mosques, the fight grewp up. On the occasion of the *Çınar vakası*[58] in March 1656—the Janissary's uproar against the bad financial management of the corpse, where the sipāhīs demanded the heads of thirty court and governement officials—the *Ḳāżızādelīs* came to be accused of corruption and to be associated with those who had worked to change the debasing the coinage. Both for this reason and because they resisted the appointment of a new grand vizier in April of 1656, from that moment, their impact on the Ottoman power structure began to decline.[59] However they tried again, at the time of the appointment of Köprülü Meḥmed Pāşā (d 1661)[60] in September 1656, to destroy all Sufi institutions. After asking advice of the *'ulamā'* about this purpose, the new grand vizier

---

56. Mehmet İpşirli and, Mustafa Uzun, 'Bahâî Mehmed Efendi', in *DİA*, 4 (1991): 463–464; B Lewis, 'Bahā'ī Meḥmed Efendi', in *E.I.*², t. I, 1960, 943.

57. 'Abd'ül-Eḥad Nūrī Efendi was born in Sivas in 1594, and educated in both the classical Islamic sciences and esoteric sciences. In Istanbul, he followed his uncle and, in Limni, performed as a *şeyh* in the Halvetī Order and as a preacher. He left about 32 works, some of which are related to the Sufi practices involved in the debate. Baz, İbrahim, *Abdülehad Nûrî-si Sivâsî. Hayatı, Eserleri, Görüşleri* (Istanbul: İnsan Yayınları, 2007), 294–295; Abdülahad Nuri Efendi, *Risaletün fi Hakki Devraniş-Sufiyye*, in Doğmuş, 128–131

58. Münir Aktepe, '*Çınar vaḳası*', in *DİA*, 8 (1993): 301–302.

59. Abdülkadir Özcan, 'Boynueğri Mehmed Paşa', in *DİA*, 6 (1992): 316–317.

60. Mücteba İlgürel, 'Köprülü Mehmed Paşa', in *DİA*, 26 (2002): 258–260; M Tayyib Gökbilgin, and RC Repp, 'Köprülü', in *EI*², V (1986): 254–256.

refused their request. Subsequently, he found that the Sultan preferred the execution of the leaders of the *Ḳāżızādelīs* movement, but instead the vizier convinced him to exile Üsṭüvānī to Cyprus. With this, the second wave of the *Ḳāżızādelīs*' struggle to impose their values on Ottoman society came to an end.

The rise of Vānī Meḥmed Efendi (d 1685)[61] to power marked the beginning of the third wave of *Ḳāżızādelī* party whose leader was able to achieve an unprecedented level of power and influence, and so he could simply succeed in banning Sufi acitivites. His opponent, Niyāzī Mıṣrī was one of the Sufis who rose to the challenge of repulsing the attacks of Vānī Meḥmed and his supporters:[62] he is a representative of the seventeenth-century struggles that wracked the Ottoman Empire, and embodied a form of Sufi dissent and acted as a partisan of the opposition to the puritanical movement of the *Ḳāżızādelī*.[63]

In 1077/1666–67, Vānī was able to ban, via a *firman* issued by the reigning sultan, the *devrān* and the *semā*ʿ. It proved to be the first time in Ottoman history that such a decision was taken on a formal and

61. Born in the province of Van in Eastern Anatolia, Vānī Efendi left this region to settle in Tabriz, and then in Erzurum where he began to preach in different mosques. Invited to the capital, in 1663, by the grand vizier Köprülü Fāżıl Aḥmed Pāṣā (d 1676), Vānī became the preacher at the Yeñi Câmiʿ Mosque before being appointed as the tutor of the son of the Sultan. After the death of the grand vizier, however, Vānī began to lose his popularity, which declined precipitously after the failed campaign of Vienna in 1683. He spent his final years near Bursa, where he died in 1685. His principal work, the *Muhyi'l ve mumīt-Sunna al-bidʿa*, is a strong refutation of practices he deemed innovations, including many Sufi practices. Öztürk, 271–281.

62. Semiramis Çavuşoğlu, *The Kâdîzâdeli Movement: An attempt of şeri'at-minded reform in the Ottoman Empire* (PhD diss, Princeton University, 1990), 168.

63. Born in 1618 in a village near Malatya, Niyāzī Mıṣrī joined the Halvetiye and began to travel from Eastern Anatolia to Baghdad and from there to Egypt where he met the Ḳādiriye. When the *semā*ʿ and *devrān* were banned by the *Ḳāżızādelī* leadership, he was a public preacher in the Aya Sofya mosque in the Ottoman capital. After an appointment in Edirne, he was subsequently exiled, first to Rhodes on account of his doctrines about the esoteric sciences, then later to Lemnos where he remained until 1692. Afterwards, he attached himself to the Ottoman campaign against Austria, but because of his rebellious statements, he was again exiled to Lemnos in 1694, where he died the same year. Niyazī was a prolific author, and he also wrote a *Risāle-i fī devrān Sūfiye*. Mustafa Aşkar, *Niyazî-i Mısrî. Hayatı, Eserleri, Görüşleri* (Istanbul: Insan Yayınları, 2004); Derin Terzioğlu, *Sufi and dissident in the Ottoman Empire: Niyâzî Misrî (1618–1694)* (PhD diss, Harvard University, 1999).

authoritarian level. According to the Mevlevī historians Sāḳıb Muṣṭafā Dede (d 1735),[64] a Mevlevī historian who left a work fundamental for understanding the history of his order, and also Ṣahīḥ Aḥmed Dede[65] and Esrār Muḥammad[66], thousands of Mevlevīs died out of sadness at this political and religious decision.[67] In Mevlevī memory, this event was recorded as the 'evil interdiction' (*yasāġ-i bed*),[68] because the law forbade any Mevlevī celebrations (*muḳābele-i 'ayin*) from taking place. Indeed, the *firman* forbade not only the *semā'* but also the sufi practice of *ẕikr* (*ẕikr cehrī*), the recitation of the *ṣahāda* (*tahlīl*) and the litany of names of God (*tasbīḥ*), while carrying the coffin of a dead Muslim. The authorities were able to prohibit, by force, the expression of these practices, while the population related to Sufi-compliance with this decision.

During the year in which the ban on *semā'* and *ẕikr* was enacted, some natural disasters occurred in various parts of the Empire shortly before the ban was pushed through, which the *Ḳāżızādelī* claimed had proved the righteousness of Vānī's position. At that time, some fanatics also attempted to destroy some of the tombs of saints that the people used to visit as a part of their devotional activities. These activities were considered idolatry (*ṣirk*) by the *Ḳāżızādelī* leaders and attempts to forbid these practices were made through an imperial decree in 1667. This proved to be the peak of the aggressive actions against Sufism and other forms of popular religious practices. The ideology tended toward violence and attacks were launched against anything that could lend itself to a public show of condemnation. Even a simple displacement from a tekke to another was enough for recreate a kind of public puritanical order.[69]

64. Sāḳıb Muṣṭafā Dede, *Sefīne-i nefīse-i Mevleviyyan* (Cairo: Bulaq, 1283/1866–67), vol. I, 180.

65. Ahmed Seyyin Sahîh Dede, *Mevlevîlerin Tarihi. Mecmûatü't-Tevârîhi'l-Mevleviyye*, translated by Cem Zorlu (Istanbul: İnsan Yayınları, 2003), 313.

66. Esrar Dede, *Tezkire-i şu'arâ-yı Mevelviyye, Inceleme-Metin*, edited by İlhan Genç (Ankara: Atatürk Kültür Merkezi Başkanlığı Yayınları, 2000), 334.

67. Necdet Yılmaz, *Osmanlı Toplumunda Tasavvuf. Sûfîler, Devlet ve Ulemâ (XVII. Yüzyıl)* (Istanbul: Osmanlı Araştirmaları Vakfi, 2001), 260; Esrar Dede, 335–337.

68. Abdülbâki Gölpınarlı, *Mevlânâ'dan Sonra Mevlevîlik* (Istanbul: İnkılâp ve Aka, 1983), 167.

69. John J Curry, *Transforming Muslim Mystical Thought in the Ottoman Empire : The Case of the Şa'bâniyye Order in Kastamonu* (Phd, The Ohio State University, 2005), 355–362.

However, after the failed siege of Vienna in 1683, people who had supported the *Ḳāżızādelī* faction became increasingly focused on more urgent issues. The death of Vānī Efendi in 1685 permanently weakened the aggressive policies aimed against practices deemed to be reprehensible innovations.

Conclusion

In sum, it is important that we not just dismiss Anḳaravī as another seventeenth-century Sufi shaykh who offered rebuttals to the intransigent *Ḳāżızādelī*–minded preachers and scholars of his time. As we have seen, the debate against sufi practices after the Anḳaravī's time becomes more and more fierce. This fact means that, at the time of Galata's shaykh there was en equilibrium in the midst of the doctrinal arguments. Even if we can not judge the work of Anḳaravī with the knowledge of the next history, we can anywere affirm with more decision that his position and his interpretations reflect the step of his own time's debate. His teachings were at the same time for giving some answer to the puritanical party's member and mostly for his disciples. It was part of his project, of course, to demonstrate an important synthesis between Sufi doctrines and Islamic law and symbolism to meet the challenges raised by the enemies of the mystical paths, but his teachings survived far beyond his own time because his Sufi wisdom extended beyond just this task. His opting for a symbolical interpretation, and for explanations according to the tradition, was a good answer to give to the detractors of Sufi practices.This is why, when we jump to the twentieth century, one of the last great master of the Mevlevī order, Meḥmed Bahāeddīn Veled Çelebi (d 1953), after having listed nine essential elements of the order in his personal notes, simply affirmed: 'Concerning the Mevlevī training, the great commentator of the *Mesnevī,* Anḳaravī Dede, has a book entitled *Minhāc'ül-fuḳarā*",[70] Implying that his followers should simply consult this work rather than have him explain it to them himself. This remark could be interpreted as laconic in nature. However, it ultimately confirms the critical place that Anḳaravī's thought established in Mevlevī cultural life.

70. Veled Çelebi İzbudak, *Tekke'den Meclis'e. Sıra Dışı Bir Çelebinin Anıları* (Istanbul: Timaş Yayınları, 2009), 143.

A Forum for Theology in the World Vol 6 No 2/2019

The Library of the Whirling Dervish: An Editorial Policy

Only a part of the abundant literature concerning Rûmî and the whirling dervishes had the honour of making it into print in the Ottoman Empire during the nineteenth century. This article aims to analyse the editorial choices guiding the selection of publications for printing within Ottoman borders.

The attempt to list this material, printed during the modern period of the Mevlevî Order's history, led us to examine the concept of the 'ideal library' for a Mevlevî Dervish—and this ideal is what we wish to reconstitute in this article. As we undertake this reconstruction, we must nevertheless remember that some works continued to be disseminated in manuscript form, even in the nineteenth century, and that within the confines of the Sufi lodge reading had always played an essential role in conferring esoteric knowledge. Thus, the advent of printed books brought about a quantitative increase (only) in the social impact of Mevlevî spirituality (as was also the case for other religious traditions). However, knowing which editorial choices were made gives us valuable clues as to the perceived ideal construction of the doctrine, and also about the history of Rûmî's Order. The introduction of printing in the Ottoman Empire was favourable to the dissemination of Sufi literature[1]—Rûmî and the dervishes do not

1. Frédéric Hitzel, 'Manuscrits, livres et culture livresque à Istanbul', in *Revue des mondes musulmans et de la Méditerranée* (1999): 88–89, 19–38; *Cumhuriyet Öncesi ve Sonrası Matbaa ve Basın Sanayii*, edited by Alpay Kabacalı (Istanbul: Cem Ofset, 1988); Johann Strauss, 'Les livres et l'imprimerie à Istanbul (1800–1908)', in P Dumont, editor, *Turquie, livres d'hier, livres d'aujourd'hui*, (Strasbourg-Istanbul, 1994), 5–24; Neri Akbayar, 'Osmanlı Yayıncılığı ', *Tanzimat'tan Cumhuriyet'e Türkiye Ansiklopedisi* (Istanbul: Iletişim Yay, 1985), 6, 1679–1696.

escape the law of modernity, by which the printed word gives birth to events. Thereafter, Mevlevî works were reproduced in ever more numerous Ottoman printing houses, either in the capital, or in Cairo (the Bulaq press), or in Anatolian cities such as Sivas and Bursa. The first printed book of Mevlevî inspiration was published by Bulaq in 1835: Ankaravî's (d 1631) commentary on the *Mesnevî*, combined with Rûmî's *Mesnevî* itself[2].

Besides this inspiring masterpiece, the first work referring to the traditions of the Mevlevî Order ever to be published in Istanbul itself was Esrâr Dede's *Dîvân*, in 1841. And thus, in the period from 1835 to approximately 1924–25, when the pamphlet *Birbirimizi Kırmayalım* was published, we can see the whirling dervish's ideal library of printed books forming (even without taking into account the significant presence of such literature in the Sufi press).[3] The banning of the Sufi Orders in 1925 and the reform of the Turkish alphabet in 1928 constitute a clear historical break which isolates new generations from the ancient Ottoman tradition. This rupture is also what caused the trace of the true Sufi Mevlevî lodge (*tekke*) library to be lost, since after 1925 the libraries of the *tekkes* were transferred to large Istanbul libraries. And so it is now difficult to reconstitute what would have been available in Sufi lodges in terms of the numbers of manuscripts or printed works.

---

2. Jalâl-Od-Dîn Rûmî, *Mathnawî. La Quête de l'Absolu*, translated by Eva de Vitray-Meyerovitch and Mortazavi Djamchid (Genève: Éditions du Rocher, 1990). The *Mesnevi* is a poem with more than twenty-five thousand verses, a veritable *Summa Theologica*. Composed of different literary genres, it is an atypical Quranic commentary (*tefsîr*). It contains anecdotes, apologetics, quotations from the Quran and from the Prophet's tradition (*Sunna*), as well as moral and hagiographic tales. This is why the mystical poet Jâmî (d 1492) described it as 'the Persian Quran'.
3. An analysis of Sufi newspapers, such as *Ceride-i sufiyye*, published in Istanbul at the beginning of the twentieth century, and *Muhibban*, published in Istanbul after the second constitution, would require considerable space, and would focus more specifically on the revelation of Mevlevî doctrine rather than on the construct of an idealised library of printed material.

Some basic work to begin the analysis of this mass of information has started recently in Turkey, but this work provides only part of the data-base[4], and we propose to present it here and enlarge upon it.

The method entails a detailed presentation and a rigorous analysis. We start with the concept of what one could consider to be the ideal Mevlevî legacy, and we then organise the whole of the literary production inspired by the Mevlevî tradition in three separate genres: those covering the life and works of Rûmî, those touching on the history of the Mevlevî Order, and finally the commentaries on Rûmî's masterpiece, the *Mesnevî*. These categories, which have been used by a number of Turkish specialists, may not encompass all of Mevlevî Sufism, but they are nevertheless a useful guide as we wander through the stacks of the ideal dervish library. Within each category, we shall present the works which were actually published in printed form, after listing those which remained only as manuscripts. We shall also give the place and date of publication, so that conclusions may be drawn as to the editorial choices that were made, while taking the contemporary political evolution of the Ottoman Empire into consideration.

Rûmî and Devout Hagiography

Since Mevlânâ Celâleddin Rûmî's death in 1273, his life has been the subject of numerous hagiographies. His earthly existence, as extraordinary as it was inspiring for his disciples, is described in various sources, in more detail than the lives of many other Persian Sufis of the Middle Ages. The famous whirling dervishes (the Mevlevîs), members of the Order founded by Rûmî and his son, have kept alive his literary, hagiographic and doctrinal tradition. The

4. Jale Baysal, *Osmanlı Türklerinin Bastıkları Kitaplar. 1729–1875 (Kitapların Tam Listesi ile)*, edited by Hasan S Keseroğlu and İlkim Mengülerek (Istanbul: Hiperlink, 2010); Ali Temizel, *Mevlâna. Çevresindekiler, Mevlevîlik ve Eserleriyle İlgili Eski Harflı Türkçe Eserler, Selçuk Üniversitesi*, Mevlâna Araştırmaları ve Uygulama Merkezi, 2009; *Mevlâna Bibliografyası/Bibliography of Mawlana*, edited by Acar Tuncel, Akıncı Sema (Ankara: Millî Kütüphane Başkanlığı yayınları, 2007); Önder, Mehmet, Binark, İsmet and Sefercioğlu, Nejat, *Mevlâna bibliyografyası*, 2 volumes (Ankara: Türkiye İş Bankası Kültür Yayınları, 1974); A Karaismailoğlu, S Okumuş. and F Coşguner, *Mevlânâ Bibliografyası* (Konya : Konya Valiliği İl Kültür ve Turizm Müdürlüğü, 2006).

Mevlevîs, following the example of their founder, have produced a very rich line of Sufi spiritual writers.[5]

Let us begin with a list of manuscript hagiographies which 19th Century publishers chose either to publish, or to leave unpublished. The first, the *İbtidaname* or *Mesnevi-i Veled*, is a chronicle written by Rûmî's son, Sultân Veled (d 1312).[6] The composition of this hagiography by Rûmî's son reveals how the holiness of a family is constructed; this holiness will, over time, become an important aspect of the Brotherhood. Along with Sipehsalâr b. Ahmed Feridun's *Risale-i Sipehsalâr*, which was completed about sixty years after the death of Rûmî,[7] this poetical work forms the prototype of Mevlevî hagiography. Rûmî's biography by Şemseddin Ahmed Eflâkî (d 1360) *Menâkıb al-ârifîn*, was composed at the request of Sultân Veled's son, Ulu Ârif Çelebi (1272–1320).[8] Between 1476 and 1478, 'Abd al-Rahmân Jâmî (d 1492), wrote an anthology of biographical notices of Sufis entitled *Nefahat al-Üns*[9], which features Rûmî and his

5. There are numerous publications, in many languages, on Rûmî, his life and work. See AF Ambrosio, E Feuillebois, and Th Zarcone, *Les derviches tourneurs. Doctrine, histoire et pratiques* (Paris: Les Editions du Cerf, 2006); Leili Anvar-Chenderoff, *Rûmî* (Paris: Editions Entrelacs, 2004); Franklin D Lewis, *Rumi. Past and Present, East and West. The Life, Teaching and Poetry of Jalâl al-Din Rumi* (Oxford: Oneworld Publications, 2000); Abdülbâki Gölpınarlı, *Mevlânâ'dan sonra Mevlevilik*, (Istanbul: İnkılâp ve Aka, 1983).
6. Bahaeddin Muhammed Veled Sultan Veled, *İbtida-name*, Turkish translation by Abdülbaki Gölpınarlı (Konya : Konya Turizm Derneği, 1976).
7. Ahmad Sipehsâlâr Ferîdûn, *Zendegînâme-i Mevlânâ celâl ed-Dîn Mowlawî* (Teheran: Eqbāl, 1946). The first translation into Ottoman Turkish, the *Tercüme-i Menâkıb-ı Mevlâna*, was by Kemâl Ahmed Dede (d 1601), a dervish who lived in the shadow of the tree in the cloister of the Mevlevî *tekke* of Yenikapı. *Cf* Akpınar, Şerife, 'Kemâl Ahmed Dede ve Tercüme-i Menâkıb-ı Mevlânâ'sı', in *Selçuk Üniversitesi Sosyal Bilimler Enstitüsü Dergisi*, 16 (2006): 35–43. Mecdüddin Feridun b Ahmed Sipehsalar, *Mevlana ve etrafındakiler: risale*, Turkish translation by Tahsin Yazıcı (Istanbul: Tercüman Gazetesi, 1977); Sipehsâlar Mecdüddin Feridun, *Risale-i Sipehsâlâr Hazreti Mevlânâ'nın Menkibeleri*, Rûmî Yayınları, 2005.
8. Clement Huart, *Les Saints des derviches tourneurs* (Paris: Ernest Leroux, 1918-1922), 2 volumes; John O'Kane *The Feats of the Knowers of God (Manâqeb al-'arefîn)* (Leiden: Brill, 2002).
9. Ebü'l-Berekat Nureddin Abdurrahman b. Ahmed b. Muhammed Cami, *Nefehatü'l-üns: evliya menkıbeleri*, Turkish translation by Mahmud B Os Lamii Çelebi, edited by Uludağ Süleyman and Kara Mustafa (Istanbul: Marifet Yayınları, 1995).

close disciples. Towards the end of the fifteenth century, Devletşâh (d 1495), wrote his *Tezkire-i şuara*, an anthology of biographies which served many orientalists as the basis for their knowledge of Rûmî.[10]

In the Turkish and Ottoman domain, the first biography of Rûmî and his disciples goes back to the beginning of the fifteenth century (1400–1401). It is the *Mahzenü'l-esrâr tercümesi*, by Zâhid b. 'Ârif, a poet of the Mevlevî Order who lived at the end of the fourteenth and the beginning of the fifteenth century. His work is a translation in verse of Aflâkî's hagiography, with additions of the translator's own composition. In 1504 the Mevlevî poet Lokmânî Dede (d 1519) composed a hagiographic poem, the *Menâkib-i Mevlânâ*, inspired by the works of Sipehsâlar and Aflâkî. Lokmânî's work was given to the Sultân Bayezid II (1448–1512) on the occasion of a trip to the capital.[11]

Subsequently, Mevlevî hagiographies in Ottoman language started to be produced at an extremely rapid pace. At the beginning of the sixteenth century, a dervish from the Konya *tekke*, Senâ'î Halîl, who died in 1543, composed the *Tercüme-i Menâkib-i sevâkib*. It was a verse translation, augmented by some original composition, of the work by 'Abdülvehhâb b. Muhhammed el-Hemedânî, and was presented as a gift to Sultân Süleyman (1494–1566). In 1589/90, Mesnevîhân Derviş Mahmûd (d 1601–02), a dervish who had been born in Konya and had joined the Mevlevî path under the guidance of Şeyh Abdüllatif (son of Sinân Dede), composed the *Tercüme-i Sevâkibü'l-menâkib*. This work—like the others cited above—is a translation of the *Sevâkibü'l-menâkib*, a Persian language resumé of Aflâkî's hagiography by 'Adbülvehhâb b. Celâleddîn Muhammad (d 1547). This Mesnevîhân Derviş Mahmûd's work was printed in 1864 by the publisher Karahisarî el-Hâc Rıza Efendi, together with the *Müzekkiü'n-nüfûs* by 'Abdülbâkî b. Eşref-i Rûmî.

'Ilmi Dede (d 1611–12) is the author of a *Menâkib-i Hazret-i Mevlânâ*, which he composed on the basis of other hagiographies. Then there is Kemâl Ahmed Dede (d 1615), who had been a dervish in Konya, under the tutelage first of Hüsrev Çelebi and then of his son Ferruh Çelebi. He is said to have arrived in Istanbul in 1591, and

10. Devletşah, *Tezkiretü'ş-şuara*, 2 volumes. Turkish translation by Lugal Necati (Ankara: Milli Eğitim Bakanlığı, 1967).

11. The publication of Lokmânî is recent, and the transcription of the work into Latin characters proves that it was never printed during the Ottoman period.

to have been the first master of the Yenikapı *tekke* there. He left the *Tercüme-i Menâkib-i Mevlânâ*, which is a translation of Aflâkî's work.

At the beginning of the eighteenth century, Anbârîzâde Derviş 'Alî b Ismâ'îl, who was born in Istanbul, learns calligraphy from the masters of the time. Inspired by several hagiographies and by Sürûrî's commentary on the *Mesnevî*, he composes the book *Esrârü'l-'ârifîn ve sirâcü't-tâlibîn*, which describes (in three introductions and twelve sections) the life of Rûmî, and the early development of the *semâ* after the death of the founder. In 1795, Gevrekzâde Hâfiz Hüseyin b. 'Abdullâh composes the *Tercüme-i Menâkibü'l-'ârifîn*; and two years later in 1797, 'Abdülbâkî Nâsir Dede composes a work by the same title. This 'Abdülbâkî Nâsir Dede, born in Istanbul in 1765, was the son of Kütahyalı Şeyh Seyyîd Ebübekir Dede, who was the *şeyh* of the Yenikapı *tekke*. In that lodge, 'Abdülbâkî Nâsir Dede had learned Arabic and Persian and became the *semâzenbaşı,* that is to say the person responsible for the dervishes who perform the ritual dance during the *semâ* ritual.

Among the Turkish translations of Persian works which remained in manuscript form, and for which the date of composition is unknown, there are a few for which we can at least name the author. One of these is the *Tercüme-i Menâkibü'l-'ârifîn*, by Korkuzâde Hâfiz Hasan. Mehmed Reşîd Çelebi, a descendant of Rûmî's family, and probably *şeyh* of the Afyon lodge, is the author of the *Tercüme-i Menâkib-i Sipehsâlar*. There are still, in the collections of Turkish libraries, other manuscript works with similar titles, which have remained anonymous. In general, the works mentioned above are closely related to the original hagiographies which served as models—as indicated by their titles. All the same, one might wonder about the need for so many different Turkish translations of Persian works. Why not circulate a single translation copied many times? This single fact inclines us to suppose that each *tekke,* or each Sufi group, felt the need to compose its own hagiographies or translations of works it considered classics or essential works of reference. An in-depth comparison of these '*tercüme*' with their originals might help us to discover the Ottoman understanding of official hagiography. But this would lead us away from our stated goal—to trace editorial choices guiding the selection of works to be printed—and invite us to study instead the process of transmission of this model of holiness in Ottoman Turkey (and consequently its reception).

In contrast, at the beginning of the twentieth century, only four books within the domain of hagiographies were printed in the Ottoman Empire. In 1900, Hocazâde Ahmed Hilmi, about whom we know very little, composes a work entitled *Silsile-i meşâyhi-i Mevleviye*. It was printed in 1900, as a medium-sized book of sixty-four pages, by the publishing house *Şirket-i Mürettebiye* in Istanbul. Between 1912 and 1913, Avni Konuk, the last great Turkish commentator of the *Mesnevî* at the end of the nineteenth century and the beginning of the 20th, writes a 144-page book entitled *Menâkib-i Hazret-i Mevlânâ Celâleddîn-i Rûmî*, which was immediately published in Istanbul, by Arşak Garuyan in 1912–1913. There was also Ahmed Mithat Bahâri Hüsâmî Beytur, who was born in Istanbul, and had been a follower of the *Mesnevî* commentaries composed by Hüseyin Fahreddîn Dede, from the Bahariye *tekke*. Although he held various government positions, he also devoted himself to composing several works on Sufism. In 1913, he translated the Aflâkî's *Tercüme-i Risâle-i Sepehsâlâr*, and it was printed as a 216-page book the same year by the *Selanik* press in Istanbul. Finally, Abdullah Cevdet (d 1932) composed a small book (only forty-nine pages) entitled *Dilmestî-i Mevlânâ*, which was published by the Orhaniye press in Istanbul in 1921.

Among the thirteen hagiographies which have been recorded, only four were published in printed form at the beginning of the twentieth century. During the nineteenth century (the focus of this paper) there was little interest in printing hagiographies of Rûmî; at that time, hagiographies were probably transmitted orally, in the Sufi lodges. The masters, by translating the principal works of their brotherhood, transmitted them to their disciples. Even though printing had been introduced in the Ottoman Empire, the traditional esoteric teaching method remained in place.

Another category of works, similar in genre to hagiographies, yet slightly different, is that of writings devoted to Rûmî's spiritual states. 'Alî Haydar Bey, who had been *kadi* in Kütahya and had then moved to Istanbul (where he died in 1914–15), composed the *Şerefnûmâ*, which was printed in Bursa (in 1888–89) by the *Ferâizci-zâde* publishing house.

The *Mevlânâ Celâleddîn-i Rûmî ve Şemseddîn-i Tebrîzî*, by Sâlih Sâ'im Unar was printed in Istanbul in 1894-95 by the '*Âlem* publishing house.

As for the twentieth century, we must mention the *Tarîhçe-i aktâb*, published in 1915 in Damascus by the publisher *eş-Şarki*. This small book, containing only 16 pages, was written by Ahmed Remzi Akyürek, one of the last great Mevlevîs, and last *şeyh* of the Üsküdar lodge. He was the son of Süleyman Ataullah Efendi, *şeyh* of the Mevlevî *tekke* of Kayseri. On his arrival in Istanbul, he became a disciple of the master of the Yenikapı *tekke*, Celâleddin Efendi, before returning to Kayseri, and from there travelling to many other destinations. In 1919, he was named *şeyh* of the Üsküdar *tekke*, and in 1925 became director of the Selimağa library. He spent some time in Ankara working in the manuscript section of the National Library, then returned to Kayseri where he died in 1944. His *Tarîhçe-i aktâb* can be seen as a supplement to the history written by Nesîb Seyyid Yûsuf Dede, who had died in 1714. In 1917–18, 'Osman Behcet published a fifty-one-page book, the *Mevlânâ Celâleddîn-i Rûmî, Hayatı ve Mesleği*, at *Evkaf* publishing house in Istanbul.

To conclude our analysis of these works which treat of Rûmî's spiritual states, we note that they represent a literary genre which appeared in the last years of the nineteenth century, towards the very end of the Ottoman Empire; the four works just mentioned were written within a thirty-year period, and all of them did see publication. This simple fact demonstrates the extent to which this era of political and civic reforms also led to, or at least revealed, a new devotional ardour (unless it was, rather, a pious renewal).

The prayers (*evrâd*, *dua*) which are the basis of Mevlevî spirituality and Sufi rituals, are also a literary genre which can be associated with the domain of devotion to the Master. At the beginning of the nineteenth century, 'Alî Feyzî b. 'Osmân translated into Turkish the book of prayers unto Mevlânâ under the title of *Tercüme-i suğra*. This was a prose translation of the prayers of Mevlânâ, which had been commissioned by Süleyman Ağa. Şeref-zâde Mehmed Fâzıl Paşa had it published, with a general commentary in 1866, by the Istanbul publishing house of Bosnavî Muharrem Efendi, as a 458-page book entitled *Şerh-i Hakâyik-i ezkâr-ı Mevlânâ*. In the same year, a certain Nûrî publishes an anthology of addresses and speeches attributed to Mevlânâ, with the title of *Münâcât-ı Hazret-i Mevlânâ*. Then there is Veled Çelebi İzbudak, who died in 1953. He was one to the last great figures of Mevlevî Sufism at the end of the Ottoman empire, and witnessed the transition toward a republican Turkey and the end of the Mevlevî Order. He devoted a great part of his life to the study and translation of Rûmî's works. The journal *Ceride-i Sufiyye* published several articles by him, containing his commentary on Mevlânâ's spiritual testament, the *Hayrü'l-kelâm*. In 1915, these articles were published as a 75 page book by the Istanbul press *Necm-i İstikbal*. At the beginning of the twentieth century, Tahirü'l-Mevlevî, who died in 1951 and was a Mevlevî personality during the final days of the Ottoman empire, published a translation of the *Münâcât-ı Hazret-i Mevlânâ* and in 1927 Ahmed Mithat Bahâri Hüsâmî Beytur, who was born in 1878–79, publishes the *Deste gül*, a book of prayers and mystical thought, attributed to Rûmî. This fort-eight-page book is printed in Istanbul by the *Sebat* press. We must note that by this date, the Sufi Orders had already been banned by the Grand National Assembly of Turkey, at the instigation of Atatürk himself. This publication comes out at a particularly interesting moment, after the banning of Sufi Orders but one year before the reform of the alphabet, which was changed from the Arabic-Persian alphabet typical of the Ottoman language to the Latin alphabet. This publication makes possible a fresh historical analysis of the time following the banning of Sufi Orders. Devotional literature probably provided a tool for the transmission of tradition, and contributed to the survival of the esoteric universe.

In summary, between the nineteenth and twentieth centuries, we see that four books of prayers were composed by Mevlevî authors, and that all were actually published during that period. This new information can be added to the partial conclusions drawn earlier: the publication of Mevlevî texts in the nineteenth century is more active in the creation of a specifically Sufi devotion.

After hagiography and devotion, poetry is most certainly a literary genre dear to Mevlevî spirituality, and was considered especially well-suited to describing or praising Rûmî's work and holiness. Rûmî's son was the first to write Mevlevî poetry. His *Dîvân-ı Tûrkî-i Sultân Veled*, besides his works in Persian, is an essential text to understand the Anatolian context and the influence of Rûmî's holiness on his contemporaries. In the following centuries however, the preferred method of transmission was hagiography—which could of course be written in verse—rather than purely poetic texts. Another text that was published in the nineteenth century is the *Medâyih-i Hazret-i Mevlânâ Muhammed Celâleddîn* by Kuddûsî Ahmed Dede (d 1849 or 1888). Kuddûsî, who was born in Niğde, belonged first to the Nakşbendiye Order and later to the Kadiriye.[12]

Among the poetic works not printed until the nineteenth century is the *Dîvân-ı Esrâr Dede* by Esrâr Mehmed Dede, who lived during the eighteenth century. This poem in Ottoman Turkish consists of thirty-six thousand couplets and was published in 1841 by the *Takvîm-i Vekâyi'* Press in Istanbul. The volume also contains two other works by the same author, the *Mübârek-nâme-i Esrâr*, and the *Fütüvvet-nâme-i Esrâr*. These last two titles focus more on the practices of the Order, expressed in poetical verses. In the *Mübârek-nâme*, Esrâr Dede also undertakes to present an esoteric interpretation of the ritual *semâ* dance. Then a few decades later, the earlier writer Hasan Nazîf Dede (who had died in 1794) is honoured by being published. Hasan, a Mevlevî poet and *şeyh* of the Beşiktaş *tekke*, had written several prose works on his Order, but also a poem, the *Divânçe* (*Meşâyih-i Mevlânâ*) and the *Ta'rîfüs'-sülûk*, more doctrinal in theme. This last work was published in Istanbul in 1859–60. Then we have Tahirü'l-Mevlevî, who died in 1951. In 1897, his *Mir'ât-ı Hazret-i Mevlânâ* is published by the Cemal Efendi Press.[13]

In 1897–99, Vasıf, a nineteenth century poet, publishes a two volume work, the *Mecmû'a-i medâyih-i Hazret-i Mevlânâ*. The first volume is 80 pages long and is published in 1897–98 by the *'Âlem* Press, and the second, 30 pages long, is published in 1898-99, also in Istanbul, by the *'Asr* Press. Finally, the *Dîvân-ı Tûrkî-i Sultân Veled,* by Veled Çelebi İzbudak, mentioned above, was edited by Kilisli Muallim Rifat (d 1953) and published in 1925, in Istanbul, by the *Matbaa-i Âmire* Imperial Press.

Of the six important poetic works devoted to Rûmî, four were printed during the nineteenth century. These poetic hagiographies and the beauty of their verses give the Mevlevî library a wealth of tools which contribute to maintaining the levels of devotion to the founder. Indeed these books were not read only by dervishes and Sufis; they also captured the attention of more literary readers. Keeping in mind the important fact that one does not read verse exclusively out of religious zeal, Turkish publishers at the end of the Ottoman Empire

12. His *Dîvân* is still read by, and offered for study to, the contemporary reader.
13. This small book comprises thirty pages. A reproduction of the original can currently be seen within the version in modern Turkish realised by Veysî Dörtbudak.

did not hesitate to publish books which might appeal both to Sufis and to intellectuals. In poetry, publishers did not hesitate to print ancient writers, such as the seventeenth century Hasan. Moreover, we noted that Sultân Veled's *Dîvân* was published in 1925—our reference date. One could almost say that as we move closer to contemporary times, we see more exploration of the hagiographical sources.

A Sacred History

When it comes to the transmission of tradition, works dealing with the Mevlevî Order are as important as those dealing with the "founder" Rûmî. Such writings can deal with the lives of either shaykhs or 'çelebis', the direct descendants of Mevlânâ's family.

In this genre, importance is placed on the description of Mevlevî personalities and of their lives, on the model of *Tezkire* (biographies). We must recall that for Mevlevîs, this literary genre had started with the *Gülşen-i esrar*, written in Persian by Şâhidî İbrahim Dede (d 1550). This text was not devoid of Shiite influences. The first work of this genre, the *Menâkib-i Sultan Dîvânî*, is attributed to Dîvâne Mehmed Çelebi, a Mevlevî *şeyh* who died in 1544, and who is also said to have been inclined to Shiism in the early part of his life. In the seventeenth century, the poet Nabî Yûsuf (d 1712) wrote the *Munşe'â*, which also contained three letters sent to the Çelebi. In the second half of the eighteenth century, Mehmed Emîn-i Tokâdî (d 1745), a member of the Nakşbendiye Order, wrote the *Menâkib-i Mevlânâ Behâ'eddîn*, inspired by the Mesnevî commentaries of Sarı 'Abdullâh (d 1660), and of Ismâil Ankaravî (d 1631). Then in 1796, Esrâr Mehmed Dede, who was born in 1749 in the Istanbul quarter called Sütlüce, and died in 1796, became famous as a poet and Mevlevî author. He was a *tekke* disciple of the celebrated Şeyh Galip. Esrâr Dede's literary monument, which is an essential work for Mevlevî history, is the *Tezkîre-i şu'arâ-yi Mevleviye* (Biography of Mevlevî poets). It contains more than two hundred biographical notices classed in alphabetical order, composed up until the last year of the author's life, in 1796.[14] But the reference work among all these

14. The transcription into modern Turkish of this historically important document has only very recently been published. See İlhan Genç. Esrar Dede, *Tezkire-i şu'arâ-yı Mevelviyye, İnceleme-Metin*, by İlhan Genç, Atatürk Kültür Merkezi Başkanlığı Yayınları (Ankara, 2000).

biographies is the *Mecmuatü't-Tevarîhi'l-Mevleviye*, written at the beginning of the nineteenth century by Sahîh Ahmed Dede (d 1813). Sahîh Ahmed Dede, born to a Mevlevî family, joined the Mevlevîyye in Konya, where he had gone on a pilgrimage. After some time spent in Kütahya, he reaches the Yenikapı *tekke* where he lends his services as master of the kitchens, and therefore as the person responsible for religious training. His Mevlevî history is based on classic texts from the Medieval period, by Aflâkî and others, and on texts by Ankaravî and Sakib Dede[15] from the Ottoman period, which are, by his time, also considered classic.

Among the works published in the 19th Century, we must list the Mevlevî history which to this day remains the most famous: the *Sefine-i nefîse-i Mevleviyân*, composed by Sâkıb Mustafa Dede, who died in 1735. The first volume gives a biography of each of the *çelebis*. The second reports on the lives of the Masters who headed each of the different *tekkes*, and the last volume traces the history of the dervishes. The book was published in three volumes of respectively 278, 233, and 144 pages, in Cairo, in 1866-67, by the Wahbiyya Press. A second edition was published in Damascus in 1916 by the Tarakkî Press.[16] In 1891–92, 'Alî Enver publishes, with the *Alem* letterpress, an abridged version of Esrâr Dede's work containing only 262 pages, entitled the *Semahane-i edeb*.[17] A few years later, in 1910, Tahirü'l-Mevlevî publishes his *Yenikapı Mevlevîhânesi postnişîn Şeyh Celâleddîn Efendi* at the *Mekteb-i Sanayi* Press.

When we examine the whole history of Mevlevî publishing during the nineteenth century, it appears that the subject of Mevlevî history itself was neglected. Of the eight books written on the historical evolution of the Order, only three were published during the nineteenth century. The subject will become more important during the second half of the twentieth century, after the Mevleviye no

15. This text wasn't printed in modern Turkish until 1992: Sahîh, Seyyin Ahmed Dede, *Mevlevîlerin Tarihi. Mecmûatü't-Tevârîhi'l-Mevleviyye*, Turkish version by Cem Zorlu (Istanbul: İnsan yayınları, 2003).

16. Ahmet Ari, *Mevlevilikte Bir Hanedanlık Kurucusu Sâkıb Dede ve Dîvânı* (Ankara: Akçağ Yayınları, 2003), 15–39; Ayan, Huseyin, 'Sefine-i Nefise-i Mevleviyân'a Göre Mevlevilik', in *Selçuk Üniversitesi 8. Millî Mevlâna Kongresi (Tebliğler) 6-7 Mayıs 1996*, (Konya, 1997), 37–42.

17. This work is now available in modern Turkish: Ali Enver Bey, *Mevlevî Şâirler. Sema 'hâne-i Edeb*, edited by Tahir Hafızoğlu (Istanbul: İnsan Yayınları, 2010).

longer officially existed. Two essential works, the *Tezkîre-i şu'arâ-yi Mevleviye* and the *Mecmuatü't-Tevarîhi'l-Mevleviye* have never been published: here again we find the ideal library, as it is put together through printing in the nineteenth century with all its choices and its selections, rejections, and silences.

Another domain in which printing facilitates the diffusion of texts in a way that was previously unknown is that of the doctrine and practices of Sufi Orders. In the case of this subject, in fact, there were fewer works left unprinted than works that were printed. Among the unpublished works that remained in manuscript form, we can cite 'Ârifî Ahmede Dede's (d 1724) Turkish translation (written in 1685) of a treatise by the great Syrian Sufi 'Abdülganî Nâblûsî ('Abd al-Ghanî al-Nâbulusî, 1641–1731), by the name of *Tercüme-i 'Ukûdü'l-lü'lüiye fi't-Tarîkati'l-Mevleviye* (Arab title: *Ukûdü'l-lü'lüiye fi't-Tarîkati'l-Mevleviye*). Then in 1768–69, Müstakîzâde Süleyman b. Sa'deddîn Mehmed Dede (d 1787–88), a member of the Nakşbendî Order, wrote the *Şerh-i 'İbârât*, a commentary on 'Abdülganî Nâblûsî's work as read in 'Ârifî's translation.[18] The publishers preferred to use the synthesis provided by Ankaravî, together with the *Minhâcü'l-fukarâ*, considered as the classic manual for the training of whirling dervishes, and the *Hüccetü'l-sema*, a treatise in defence of the sacred Mevlevî dance. Written in the first decades of the seventeenth century, they were twice published during the nineteenth century. Both of Ankaravî's works, which together form a cohesive whole, were published first in 1840 in Egypt, by Bûlâq, thus confirming the importance of books in Ottoman Turkish in the first period of Bûlâq publishing; they were then published a second time, in 1869, by the Rıza Efendi Press in Istanbul.[19] These editions are for the most part identical, their main difference being the pagination; however, the Istanbul edition is easier to read and slightly more handsome, with its dark green binding. This dissemination in print of Ankaravî's work is due to the presence in Cairo of a Mevlevî *tekke*, housing Turkish-speaking

18. Studies of Nâbulusî are increasingly numerous, given his importance in the religious history of the Arab provinces between the 17th and 18th Centuries. See particularly : Sirriyeh, Elizabeth, *Sufi Visionary of Ottoman Damascus. 'Abd al-Ghanī al-Nābulusī, 1641–1731* (London and New York: Routledge Curzon, 2005).

19. Alberto Fabio Ambrosio, *Vie d'un derviche tourneur. Doctrine et rituels du soufisme au XVIIe siècle* (Paris: CNRS Editions, 2010), 109–115.

dervishes. Publishing material in Ottoman Turkish in an Arabic-speaking country could only be justified if individuals from Anatolia and from the capital were actually settled in the Arab provinces of the Empire. Moreover, it is easy to imagine that these same dervishes, who travelled freely throughout the Ottoman Empire, could also offer to circulate and deliver printed books from one area to the other, and transport Ottoman-language material to Anatolia and elsewhere.

In the middle of the eighteenth century, Esrâr Mehmed Dede wrote the *Mübareknâme-i Esrâr*, his explanation of the Mevlevî spiritual concert (*semâ'*), published with his *Dîvân*. In 1864, Hâcı Feyzullâh Nakşbendî publishes in Istanbul, at the *Âmire* printing house, a small book of approximately twenty pages, entitled *İşâretü'l-ma'neviye*, on the symbolical explanation of the Mevlevî *semâ'*.[20] In 1918, Mahmûd Celâleddîn publishes at the *Şems* letter-press a twenty-seven-page book, the *Hakâyik-i semâ'*, a translation and explanation of Hâcı Feyzullâh Nakşbendî book. In 1921–22, an unknown author publishes a version of the *Risâle-i Mevlevî*, and two years later in 1923–24, the *Evkaf-ı İslâmiye* publishing house prints a twenty-nine-page pamphlet; it is the famous text *Birbirimizi Kırmayalım*, by Mehmed Veled Çelebi İzbudak. In it, the author exhorts the dervishes from various Sufi Orders not to enter into conflict with one another. Toward the end of the Ottoman Empire, the heads of Sufi Orders had been grouped in a sort of Sufi directorial committee. It is not impossible that İzbudak's intention was also to encourage communion between members of different traditions, as well as among members of the Orders of whirling dervishes.

Let us now conclude our inventory of these doctrinal works. Doctrine is very clearly appreciated among Mevlevî Sufis of the nineteenth century, as is attested by their publishing history: of the nine existing works on Mevlevî doctrine and rites, six are published during the 19th Century and the very beginning of the twentieth century. It's evident that devotion without doctrine is not in itself sufficient. Doctrinal support is necessary, and therefore the books which explain it are indispensable. Authors who were active during the empire's last years paid heed to reference works on Sufi doctrine

20. This work is now available in a modern Turkish version and in a new edition of the Ottoman Turkish text: Hâcı Feyzullah en-Nakşibendî el-Murâdî el-Mevlevî, *Mevlevî Âyini'nde Manevî İşaretler*, edited by M Akif Kuruçay, Meram Belediyesi Kültür Yayınları, 2005.

as well as to their own works of synthesis, which were probably based on classical and traditional teaching methods. One sees a sort of alliance between tradition and modern technology—in this case printing—in order to disseminate both ancient and new ideas. Modern authors also use publishing, since it is available to promote the success of their intellectual labour. At the end of the Empire, works on doctrine and religious practice are published more often, as both need to be defended against the attacks of a certain form of anti-Sufi positivism, popular among intellectuals. The re-reading of doctrines, and consequently of practices, by modern authors, and the publication of their resulting works, make for an indirect response to this intellectual movement. The Bektaşîs for instance, are subjected to the most ferocious criticism because of their suspicious rituals. And, as it was during Ankaravî's time, Sufis themselves must undertake their own defence. Printing presses support Mevlevî Sufism and the authors who devote themselves to propagating the tradition.

Sufi spaces: the *tekkes*, the *mevlevîhânes* (whirling dervish lodges), the *âsitânes*, attracted more interest at the very same time as Mustafa Kemal was proclaiming a ban on dervish Orders in 1925, thus creating a certain nostalgia for the past. It became important then to retrace the history of Sufi devotional places that had now closed their doors. But in fact, Ottoman Sufis had long been interested in the various *tekkes*, which were seen as endowed with sacred history and carrying the chain of transmission from shaykh to shaykh. The first writing of this type goes back to the end of the eighteenth century: it is a collection (*Mecmû'a*) dating from 1796. Then we have the work *Defter-i Dervîşân*, which is contained within the *Mecmû'a,* and dates in part from 1798 and in part from 1813; it presents biographical notices of all the *şeyhs* of the Yenikapı *tekke*. Its author, 'Alî Nutkî Dede (d 1804), had become Shaykh of this very lodge on the death of his father. When Nutkî in his turn died, his brother 'Abdülbâkî Nâsır Dede (d 1821) completed the *Defter-i Dervîşân.*[21] This lodge was also the subject of a history, *Yenikapı Mevlevîhânesi,* by the historian Mehmed Ziyâ (d 1930), who was himself a Mevlevî. This history

21. *Defter-i Dervîşân.Yenikapı Mevlevîhânesi Günlükleri*, edited by Bayram Ali Kaya and Sezai Küçük (Istanbul: Zeytinburnu Belediyesi Kültür Yayınları, 2011).

was published twice in Ottoman Turkish: the first time by the Şems printing press in 1910, and the second in 1913 by the Arakes press.[22]

Thus, two out of the three available documents concerning Sufi institutions were printed. Ought we to conclude from this that the history of the *tekkes* inspired editorial interest? The sample is a small one, but during the Republican period one of the principle areas of research for specialists in art history, particularly those for whom Turkish was their mother tongue, was the evolution through history of Mevlevî buildings, specifically the changes, restorations and renovations of these complexes. A new field of scientific enquiry appears to have evolved from this research, that of reflection on the symbolism of architecture. For this reason, publications from the 19th Century aroused interest during the Republican period.

Mevlevî music is a crucial element of the Sufi culture of this Order. That which is fundamental, essential, is sometimes not even recorded. This was the case for Mevlevî music (*'ayîn mevlevî*), because it was always transmitted orally. Musical notation and written parts appeared very late by comparison with the actual tradition of this music, which dates from at least the fourteenth century for the most ancient Mevlevî musics. The *Mevlevî 'âyînleri mecmû'ası*, composed in 1905, is the oldest known attempt to collect and notate the music that accompanies the celebration of the *semâ'*; although it's evident that this work is fundamental, it has never been published, even to this day.

However, in the Republican era Sufi and especially Mevlevî music enjoys a veritable retranscription, which also stirred up debates in musicology, and above all in ideology. In the last few years, at least two collections of Mevlevî music scores have appeared in print, the work of Turkish specialists in Ottoman musicology.[23] The old way of transmitting music—orally—has been abandoned in favour of modern methods, as used in traditional European music and adopted in the republican climate of contemporary Turkey.

---

22. This book was, during the Republican era, translated into modern Turkish, or transcribed into Latin characters: Ziya Bey, İhtifalci Mehmed, *Yenikapı Mevlevihanesi*, translated by Murat A Karavelioğlu, (Istanbul: Ataç Yayınarı, 2005).

23. *Beste-i Kâdim'den Beste-i Cedîd'e Mevlevi Âyînleri*, edited by Hâfız Ahmet Çalışır, Çizgi Yayınları, 2 volumes, 2010; Salgar, Fatih, *Mevlevî Âyînleri. The Music Of Divine Love* (Istanbul: Ötüken Neşriyat, *2008); Mevlevi Ayinleri,* edited by Sadettin Hepe (Konya : Konya Turizm Derneği, 1979).

The cosmos of commentaries

Among Rûmî's works, besides the Mesnevî, we must also cite the *Divan-i Şems-i-Tebriz* (the Divan of Şems), a collection of ghazals[24] (all ending with the name of Şems) and of quatrains.[25] The ghazal is a poetic form, of Arabic and Persian origin. As for Rûmî's prose writings, we should cite the miscellany of thoughts gathered by his son under the title of *Fîhi-mâ-fîhi*. It consists of a series of answers to questions posed by his disciples.[26] In addition, the *Mecalis-i seb'a* (The Sermons, literally the seven sessions) is a collection of sermons which Rûmî gave from the pulpit. These texts begin to circulate apart from Rûmî's other prose works toward the end of the first half of the fourteenth century. There are also numerous letters of circumstance from Mevlânâ, with the title of *Mektuba*.[27]

Translations of the Mesnevî into Ottoman Turkish

Soon after Rûmî's death, sections of his Mesnevî were translated into Turkish, either as edifying stories, or in the form of texts concerning

24. Published for the first time in Europe by Vincenz von Rosenzweig-Schwannau in 1838, with the translation of a selection of seventy-five poems. This was followed by RA Nicholson's translation, in 1898. Eva de Vitray Meyerovitch has also translated parts of these mystical poems: Mawlânâ Djalâl Od-Dîn Rûmî, *Odes mystiques (Dîvân-E Shams-E Tabrîzî)*, translated by Eva de Vitray-Meyerovitch and Mohammad Mokri (Paris: Editions du Seuil, Editions Unesco, 1973).
25. These were first published, in Istanbul in 1946, by Hâlet Çelebi, with a French translation. Later, Forouzanfar took over their publishing. The two thousand quatrains published by the latter were translated into French by Eva de Vitray-Meyerovitch: Mawlânâ Jalâl-Od-Dîn Rûmî, *Rubâi'yât*, translated into French by Eva de Vitray-Meyerovitch and Djamchid Mortazavi (Paris: Albin Michel, 1993 paperback, 1987).
26. Published by Forouzanfar in 1951, these discourses are available in several European languages : two translations into English—by AJ Arberry, in 1972 and by Wheeler Trackston in 1994, *Signs of the Unseen*, Putney, VT / Thresold Books. The French translation was by Eva de Vitray-Meyerovitch, Djalâl-Ud-Dîn Rûmî, 1975, *Le livre du dedans, Fihi-mâ-fîhi*, translation into French by Eva de Vitray-Meyerovitch (Paris: Albin Michel, 1997). And an Italian translation: Jalâl Ad Dîn Rûmî, *L'essenza del reale, Fîhi-mâ-fîhi, (C'è quel che c'è)*, translated by Sergio Foti (Torino: Libreria Editrice Psiche, 1995).
27. These letters, which, according to the edition published Yusuf Djamshidi et Gholâm-Huseyn Amin are 144 in number, were translated into French by Eva de Vitray-Meyerovitch; this is the only translation into a European language, Djalâl-Od-Dîn Rûmî, *Lettres*, translated by Eva de Vitray-Meyerovitch (Paris: Editions Jacqueline Renard, 1990).

religious or even Sufi practices.[28] The influence of Rûmî in literature leads one to believe that manuscript copies of his works circulated freely and were easily accessible in the Sufi and literary milieux of Anatolia.

In the years 1712 and 1730 Nahîfî Süleymân Efendi (d 1737) translates Rûmî's masterpiece into Turkish in its entirety for the first time. Nahîfî had become a disciple of the Mevlevî Order upon his return from Iran, passing through Konya. He had been named *şeyh* of the Kasımpaşa *tekke* in Istanbul. His translation respected the style and genres of the original text: verses are translated in verse and prose remains in prose. The work, in seven volumes, is published by Bulaq, in Cairo, in 1851.[29] Nahîfî is then followed by Mehmed Şakir, who between 1830 and 1835 translates all of Rûmî's masterpiece, adding to it a translation of the seventh, apocryphal, *defter*. This work remains unpublished.[30]

Partial translations into Ottoman Turkish are also fairly numerous. The first translator is Muhammad Nazmî Efendi, (d 1701)[31]: his work, the *Sırr-ı ma'nevî*, or The Spiritual Secret, is composed in 1676–77 and consists of a translation of the first book of the Mesnevî.[32]

Hayri Bey (who died in 1891) offers yet another translation, which he prefaces with criticisms of Nahîfî's translation. His book, composed in or about 1888, is published in Istanbul in 1890–91 by the Mahmut Bey Press. In 1910–11, Fazlullah Rahimî translates a selection of 124 tales from the Mesnevî, entiltled *Gülzar-ı Hakikat*.

28. For this part, I am essentially following Ismail Güleç, *Türk edebiyatında Mesnevi tercüme ve şerhleri* (Istanbul: Pan Yayıncılık, 2008); Ismail Güleç 'Türk Edebiyatında Mesnevî Tercüme ve Şerhleri', in *Journal of Turkish Studies*, 27/II (2003): 161–176; and Semih Ceyhan, 'Mesnevî', in *Türkiye Diyanet Vakfı İslâm Ansiklopedisi*, (Istanbul: Türkiye Diyanet Vakfı İslâm Araştırmaları Merkezi), volume 29, 325–334.

29. For the modern version, see: Mevlânâ Celâleddin-i Rûmî, *Mesnevî-i Şerîf*, translated by Süleyman Nahîfî, edited by Âmil Çelebioğlu (Istanbul: Timaş Yayınları, 2007).

30. Ahmet Metin Şahin has now realised a complete verse translation of this work: Muhammed b. Muhammed b. Hüseyin Mevlana Celaleddin-i Rumi, *Mesnevi*, edited by Ahmet Metin Şahin (Istanbul: Kaynak Yayınları, 2006).

31. Needet Yılmaz, *Osmanlı Toplumunda Tasavvuf: Sûfîler, Devlet ve Ulemâ (XVII Yüzyıl)* (Istanbul: Osmanlı Araştirmaları Vakfi, 2001), 212–214.

32. Muhammed Nazmî-i Halvetî, *Sırr-ı ma'nevî (Manzum Mesnevî Tercümesi)*, edited by Ekrem Bektaş, Selçuk Üniversitesi, Mevlâna Araştırmaları ve Uygulama Merkezi, 2009.

The work is composed of three volumes and is published in Istanbul by the Publishing House of the Military Medical School (*Metkeb-i Tıbbiye-i Askeriye*), which is somewhat surprising, as it is one of the most advanced military institutions for reforms and methodology which undertakes the publication of this work. These three volumes contain respectively 254, 283 (in 1910) and 346 pages (in 1911).

Finally, we must mention the publication in Tehran in 1891 of a selection of tales translated for children, entitled *Kitâb-ı Müstetâb-ı Mesnevî li'l-Eftâl,* by Miftâhü'l-Mülk Mahmud.

Commentaries on the Mesnevî

These commentaries exist in either complete or partial form. Among the latter should be cited the work of Mustafa Şem'î Dede (d 1526). After spending one night in a *tekke,* he decided to write—in Turkish—a commentary of Mevlânâ's famous poem, by the light of Truth (*hakikat*), in the secrets of the Path (*tarikat*) and in observance of the *şeriat.* His *Şerh-i Mesnevî-i Şerîf'i* is the first complete commentary of the Mesnevî. Somewhat later, Şem'î Şemu'ullah (d 1600) translates the whole poem, and writes his commentary on it.

In the seventeenth century, Şifâî Mehmed Dede (d 1671) composes, while in the Mevlevî lodge of Cairo, a complete commentary of the Mesnevî, the *Şerh-i Mesnevî-i Şerîf,* which enlarges upon the works of Sururi and Ismail Efendi. Finally, between 1839 and 1845, Murad Mehmed Efendi composes his own complete commentary, under the title of *Hulâsatü'ş-şürûh.*[33]

Complete commentaries are rare, since the work may require a lifetime to complete. Partial commentaries are more frequent; perhaps the author feels more inclined to undertake such a project if he does not feel obliged to complete the whole laborious task. Or, he may have begun the job meaning to carry it through to the end, but been obliged to stop because of the demands of the commentator's way of life; the result is the same. In the fifteenth century, in 1436, Mûîn ed-Dîn b.

33. Other, tardier commentaries were published during the twentieth century. Ahmet Avni Konuk (d 1938) composed his commentary between 1929 and 1937. Tahirü'l-Mevlevî (d 1951) created his between 1949 and 1951, Abdülbâkı Gölpınarlı's (d 1982) dates from 1972. See : Mevlânâ Celâleddîn Rûmî, *Mesnevî-i Şerîf Şerhi,* trans. and commentary A Avni Konuk (Istanbul: Gelenek Yayıncılık (for the first two volumes) and Kitabevi (III-XIII), 2004).

Mustafa, a Mevlevî poet, writes the first translation of Rûmîs' work, followed by a commentary on the first two books. This translation was offered to Sultan Murad II and thus is entitled *Mesnevî-i Muradî.*[34] We must also cite Ankaravî's partial commentaries of the Mesnevî, such as the *Fâtihu'l-Ebyat*, written prior to 1620, *Hall-i müşkiât-i mesnevî*, the *Tuhfetü'l-berere*, and the *Câmi'u'l-âyât.*

The second commentator of the first book of the *Mesnevî*, the *Mesnevî Şerhi,* is Seyyid Ebussuud b. Seyyid Sadullah el-Hüseynî, el-Kayserî, who writes his commentary between 1577 and 1578. Then there is Abdülmecid Sivâsî (d 1639). In a dream, he saw Mevlânâ, who ordered him to compose poetry about his work. Abdülmecid Sivâsî informed Sultan Ahmed the First of this dream-command and wrote the *Şerh-i Mesnevi* between 1637 and 1638. He stopped after writing the first book. During the seventeenth century, Pîr Muhammed Efendi comments on the first four *defter* in his *Hazinetü'l-Ebrâr.* A few years later, in 1694, Tâlibî Hasan translates, and comments on, the third book of the *Mesnevî*, in a work entitled *Yetîmü'ş-şürûh.* At the very end of the seventeenth century, Mehmed 'Alî el-Mevlevî translates and comments on the first book of the *Mesnevî.* His work bears the same title as the original: *Mesnevî-i Ma'nevî.*

Among the works of this sort which were published, we must cite the following: Sarı Abdullah Efendi (d 1660)[35] wrote a commentary on the first *defter*, in the years between 1625 and 1631. It is the only one that was subsequently printed, under the title *Cevahir-i Bevahir-i Mesnevi.* This work, a commentary on the first book of the *Mesnevî*, was written in five volumes and published in 1870–71 by the *Tasvîr-i Efkâr* publishing house. At the beginning of the 18th century, Hakkı Bursevî (d 1725)[36], writes *Ruh-ul-Mesnevi*[37], a commentary on 748 couplets of the *Mesnevî.* This two-volume work is printed in 1871 by the Imperial Printing House. In the 19th Century, Erzurumlu Ahmed Naim completes his commentary on the fourth book of the

34. Yavuz, Kemal, *Mu'ini'nin Mesnevi-i Muradiyye'si Mesnevi Tercüme ve Şerhi*, 2 volumes (Konya: Selçuk Üniversite Yayınları, 2007).

35. Necdet Yılmaz, *Osmanlı Toplumunda Tasavvuf. Sûfîler, Devlet ve Ulemâ (XVII. Yüzyıl)*. 345–353.

36. Ali Namlı, *İsmâil Hakkı Bursevî. Hayatı, Eserleri ve Tarîkat Anlayışı* (Istanbul: İnsan Yayınları, 2001).

37. İsmail Hakkı Bursevî, *Rûhü'l-Mesnevî—Mesnevî'nin ilk 748 beytinin şerhi-*, edited by İsmail Guleç (Istanbul: İnsan Yayınları, 2004).

Mesnevî in 1813, while Âbidin Paşa (d 1907) gives us in 1888-89 four volumes of commentary (entitled *Şerh-i Mesnevî)* on the first *defter* of the *Mesnevî*. This work would be published several times[38] both in Istanbul and in Ankara. Âbidin Paşa lived in Ankara for several years, which may explain why his commentary was published in the city which later became the capital.

Kenan Rifai (d 1950), one of the last great heirs of Ottoman Sufism, and a descendant of the founder of the Rifâiye Order, orally taught and commented on the *Mesnevî* between 1906 and 1923, but the notes taken by his disciples were published for the first time only in 1970, in Ankara.[39]

Partial commentaries on the *Mesnevî* are certainly easier to publish, and yet they do not seem to be viewed particularly favourably by editors. There are also many works of this sort which remain in manuscript form. Even when their authors are important, this type of commentary is more likely, in Sufi circles, to be transmitted orally. It is İbrahim Beg (Bey) who, in the 15th century, writes the first commentary on selections from the *Mesnevî*; it is composed of 2377

38. These are the different editions :

1st volume, Sivas, 1886, *Vilayet matbaası*, 719 + 4.
1st vol. Istanbul, 1886, *Osmaniye matbaası*
2nd vol. Ankara, 1887, *Vilayet matbaası*, 880 + 33.
3rd vol. Ankara, 1888, *Vilayet matbaası*, 678 + 7.
4th vol. Ankara, 1888, *Vilayet matbaası*, 706 + 4.
1st vol. Istanbul, 1888, *Mahmud Bey matbaası*, 499 + 7.
2nd vol. Istanbul, 1888, *Mahmud Bey matbaası*, 401 + 4.
3rd vol. Istanbul, 1888, *Mahmud Bey matbaası*, 307 + 4.
4th vol. Istanbul, 1888, *Mahmud Bey matbaası*, 327 + 1.
5th vol. Istanbul, 1889, *Mahmud Bey matbaası*, 349 + 2.
6th vol. Istanbul, 1889, *Mahmud Bey matbaası*, 384 + 2.
1st vol. Istanbul, 1908, *Mahmud Bey matbaası*, 376.
2nd vol. Istanbul, 1908, *Kütübhane-i Cihan matbaası*, 266.
3rd vol. Istanbul, 1908, *Kütübhane-i Cihan matbaası*, 296 + 2.
4th vol. Istanbul, 1909, *Kütübhane-i Cihan matbaası*, 240 + 1.
5th vol. Istanbul, 1910, *Kütübhane-i Cihan matbaası*, 254 + 2.
6th vol. Istanbul, 1910, *Kütübhane-i Cihan matbaası*, 240.

Abidin Paşa, *Mesnevî Şerhi*, edited by Mehmet Sait Karaçorlu, 2 volumes (Istanbul: İz Yayıncılık, 2007); İskender Pala, 'Abidin Paşa ', in *Türkiye Diyanet Vakfı İslâm Ansiklopedisi*, volume 1, 1988, 310.

39. Tahralı, Mustafa, 'Kenan Rifâî', in *Türkiye Diyanet Vakfı İslâm Ansiklopedisi* (Istanbul: Türkiye Diyanet Vakfı İslâm Araştırmaları Merkezi, 2002), volume 25, 254–255.

couplets (*beyt*). Because of the entreaties to God that he begins with, the work is often referred to as *Münacaat-ı Ibrahim Big*. Then in the sixteenth century, Hacı Pîrî (d 1587–88) composed a commentary on selected texts from the first *defter*, with the title of *İntihâb-ı Şerh-i Mesnevî*. Later in the century, Sûdî (who died sometime between 1592 and 1596) also left us a commentary, the *Şerh-i Mesnevî*, of which one volume was recently rediscovered.[40] Abdülmecîd Muharremn ez-Zilî (d 1617) comments on texts both from the first book of the *Mesnevî* and from the *Ceziretu'l-Mesnevi*. 'Adnî Receb Dede (d 1638) selects 339 couplets on which to comment in his *Nahl-i tecellî*. Sabuhî Ahmed b. Muhammad (d 1647), the Mevlevî Shaykh of the Yenikapı *tekke*, a Mevlevî lodge outside the old ramparts of the byzantine city, writes the *al-İhtiyarat-ı Hazret-i Mesnevi-i Şerîf*, where he comments on the foreword of each *defter*, as well as on a selection of couplets. Still in the seventeenth century, but in Galata, another part of the city, İsmail Ankaravî composes several works which contain commentaries on passages of the *Mesnevî*: *Nisâb'ül-Mevlevî*, *Câmiü'l-Âyât*, *Hall-i Müşkilât-ı Mesnevî* and *Tuhfetü'l-Berere*—all of which remain unpublished. Also unpublished were the commentary by Yenişehirli Avni Bey (d 1883) who translated the first two books of the *Mesnevî*,[41] and *Revâyihu'l-Mesnevîyât*, a work by Mehmed Emin in which he comments on a selection of texts from the first *defter*, including the first 18 verses. Later still, and still unpublished, we find the commentary on 360 couplets from the first *defter* by Es'ad Mehmed Dede, a renowned author of the early twentieth century.

The only commentaries on selected passages which had the honour of being printed are the *Müntehebât-ı Mesnevî*, by Seyyid Mehmed Şükrü, published in Istanbul by the Şems Publishing House in 1910, and, at the same period, the *Şerh-i Râsim Müntehabâtu alâ Mesnevî-yi Şerîf*, by Hocazâde Seyyid Mehmed Râsim el-Mevlevî.

Rûmî's masterpiece inspired yet another type of commentary, the first example of which was the *Ceziretü'l-Mesnevi*, written in Persian

40. Communication by Slobodan Iliç 'Rumi's *Masnavi* and the lost commentary of Sudi Bosnavi (d ca 1599)', at the conference organised by the Iranheritage Foundation: *Wondrous Words: The Poetic Mastery of Jalal al Din Rumi*, 13–15 September 2007, British Museum, London.

41. Mehmet Çavuşoğlu, 'Avnî Bey, Yenişehirli ', in *Türkiye Diyanet Vakfı İslâm Ansiklopedisi* (Istanbul: Türkiye Diyanet Vakfı İslâm Araştırmaları Merkezi), 1991), volume 4, 12–124.

by Yusuf Sineçak. It consists of a selection of 360 couplets from each book of the *Mesnevi*. With these passages, selected by Sineçak, as starting points, various writers compose commentaries. The first such commentator, who remains unpublished, is Mehmet 'İlmî Dede (d 1611); in 1571, in his *Lemeât-ı bahru'l-ma'nevî şerh-i cezire-i Mesnevi*, he composed a Turkish translation of the Persian text, as well as a commentary. A bit later, in 1602, Abdülmecid Sivâsî writes his *Şerh-i cezire-i Mesnevi*. Then we have two commentaries by Abdullah Bosnevî (d 1644):[42] the *Cezire-i Mesnevi Şerhi* and the *Şerh-i manzum-i cezire-i Mesnevi*. These two works were never published in printed form. The same fate befell the *Şerh-i Cezîre-i Mesnevî*, a commentary by Shaykh Galip Dede (d 1799); written between 1789 and 1790, it was not published until the twenty-first century. Galip Dede is one of the best-known authors of Ottoman literature, famous for his love poem *Hüsn ü Aşk*,[43] composed in 1783, which offers a symbolic Sufi interpretation of profane love.[44] The fact that some commentaries were never printed is not due only to their having been composed during the far distant past of Mevlevî history. The work of Ferid Efendi, written in 1838, also remains unpublished. On the other hand, we see that the work of Cevrî İbrahim Çelebi (d 1654), a native of Istanbul who was a disciple of Ankaravî and a Dîvân secretary, was treated differently. In 1647, he wrote *Hall-i Tahkikat* and *Aynü'l-füyuz*.[45] The first of these (of which a

42. Kara, Mustafa, 'Abdullah Bosnevî', in *Türkiye Diyanet Vakfı İslâm Ansiklopedisi* (Istanbul: Türkiye Diyanet Vakfı İslâm Araştırmaları Merkezi, 1988), volume 1, 87.
43. Editions of this work are numerous in contemporary Turkey. I would like to mention: Şeyh Galib, *Hüsn ü Aşk. Metin-Nesre Çeviri-Notlar ve Açıklamalar*, edited by Muhammet Nur Doğan (Istanbul: Ötüken Neşriyat, 2002); Şeyh Galib, *Hüsn ü Aşk*, edited by Orhan Okay and Hüseyin Ayan (Istanbul: Dergâh Yayınları, 2000), third edition. Victoria Rowe Holbrook, who has studied the works of Şeyh Gâlib, proposes a version in Turkish transcription, based on the older version by Gölpınarlı, accompanied by an English translation: Şeyh Galib, *Hüsn ü Aşk*, edited by Victoria Rowe Holbrook (New York: The Modern Language Association of America, 2005); Şeyh Galib, *Beauty and Love*, English translation by Victoria Rowe Holbrook (New York: The Modern Language Association of America, 2005).
44. Ahmet Arı, *Galib Dede'nin Aşk Ateşi Şeyh Galib Divanı'nda Aşk* (Isparta: Fakültc Kitabevi, 2003); Holbrook, Victoria Rowe Holbrook, *The Unreadable Shores of Love. Turkish Modernity and Mystic Romance* (Austin: University of Texas Press, 1994).
45. Hüseyin Ayan, 'Cevrî İbrahim Çelebi', in *Türkiye Diyanet Vakfı İslâm Ansiklopedisi*, 1993), volume 7, 460–461.

number of manuscript copies are still extent) is a commentary on the *Mesnevî* and was extremely successful. The second is a commentary on Sineçak's writings. Both were published in a single volume, in 1852–53, by the Printing House *Takvîmhâne-i Âmire*, and then again in 1898 by the *Mihran* Printing House.

We shall now study a slightly different genre, that of commentaries on the first eighteen verses of the Mesnevî only. These are, of course, the introduction to the entire work, but could also be said to present a synthesis of Rûmî's thought. At least in Mevlevî tradition, this beginning was considered the zenith of the masterpiece. Among works of this type which remain unpublished, we can cite that of İbrahim Tennurî (he died in 1482 and was affiliated with the Bayramiye-Şemsiye Order)[46] who presented to the conquering Fâtih Sultan Mehmed a work in Turkish entitled *Gülzar-ı ma'nevî*. Then we have the work of Lokmânî Dede (d 1504), who, in his hagiography mentioned earlier, offers a commentary in Turkish of the first eighteen verses of the *Mesnevî*. The same type of unpublished commentary is written by Ebu's-Senâ Şeyh Şemseddîn Ahmed es-Sivâsî, who died in 1597–98. Then we have Abdullah, who comments on some passages of the *Mesnevî* and of the *Dîvân-i Kebir*, in his *Kitâbu Kâşifü'l-Estâr an Nevâsii Mehâbîbi'l-Esrâr*, which exists only in manuscript form. The work of Abdullah Bosnevî (d 1628), *Mekâsidü Envârı Ayniyye*, which comments on 3,339 verses of the first book of the *Mesnevî*, exists only as a manuscript, as does the work of Pirî Mehmed Paşa (d 1532) who wrote the *Tuhfe-i mir*, a commentary on the work of Şâhidî and on some verses of Rûmî's. And, still in the realm of the unpublished, we must note in the seventeenth century the following works: the *Şah u kenizek*, by Ağazade (d 1652) who comments on the first eighteem verses of the *Mesnevî*; the *Esrâru'l-Arifîn ve Sirârcü't-Tâlibîn* by Dervîş Ali b. İsmail; the work by Mehmed Emin Tokâdî (d 1745) who comments on seventy-five couplets; and finally the work of Bağdatlı Âsım (d after 1888) who commented on the first eighteen verses in his Dîvân. It is somewhat surprising that commentaries on the first eighteen verses—a fundamental section of the *Mesnevî*—remained mostly unpublished.

---

46. Uzun, Mustafa, 'İbrâhim Tennûrî', in *Türkiye Diyanet Vakfı İslâm Ansiklopedisi*, volume 21, 2000, 356.

Among those which were published, we can place the following works on the shelves of the Meslevî library: the *Gülşen-i tevhid*,[47] by the Mevlevî Şâhidî İbrahim Dede (d 1550). He had a good command of the original language of Rûmî's *Mesnevî* and wrote commentaries on 100 couplets chosen from each of its books; for each couplet in the original, he composed five verses in Turkish. The *Gülşen-i tevhid* was printed in 1878. Seyyîd Emîr-i Buhârî, (d 1516) composed a commentary on a number of ghazals, and it was published in 1912 by Ahmed Kamil's Publishing House. The book, printed in Istanbul, has fifteen pages. Then in 1888, Âbidin Paşa, mentioned earlier, publishes a commentary in Turkish of some tales by Rûmî at the Mahmut Bey Publishing House. The work is entitled *Mesnevî-i Şerîf'deki Arabî Kıssası.*

Quantitative analysis of the publication of commentaries.

The analysis of the selection for publication of translations and commentaries is rather complex, in view of the various genres involved. Of two complete ancient translations in verse of the *Mesnevî*, only one is printed during the nineteenth century, the one by Nâhifî. It is in Ottoman Turkish, and close to Rûmî's verses in Persian, which explains why it was chosen for publication. One of the most popular versions in Turkey is precisely the Nâhifî translation, transposed into Latin characters. The complete prose translation, on the other hand, does not arrive until the twentieth century; this is another proof of the special affinity between Ottoman Turkish and Rûmî's language, an affinity which encouraged the wide-spread diffusion and appreciation of the verse translation. Let us not forget that the translation presented in Ankaravî's commentary was the one that permitted many readers to become acquainted with an Ottoman version of the text. Ottoman readers try to stay as close as possible in emotional and literary sensibility to the Persian original of the *Mesnevî*. Poetry is so powerful as a means of transmission that publishers of printed versions could not avoid it.

Of three partial translations of the *Mesnevî*, one only is published: these partial works do not seem to interest publishers. One might find an explanation in the idea that the *Mesnevî*, considered sacred, cannot be published in parts but must remain whole. The opposite

47. Şâhidî İbrâhim Dede, *Gülşen-i Vahdet (Yüz ile ilgili Tasavvufî Remzler)*, edited by Numan Külekçi (Ankara: Akçağ Yayınları, 1996).

pertains to commentaries on parts of the text: one might hesitate to publish only a part of the Mesnevi, but one does not hesitate to publish a partial commentary of Rûmî's glorious verses.

A study of the commentaries leads us to an even more interesting conclusion: of the eleven known works of this sort, only Ankaravî's commentary is published in the nineteenth century, and it is published several times. His interpretation almost assumes the character of an official text among Ottoman Turks. His thought, influenced by both Rûmî and Ibn 'Arabî, can be said to constitute the intellectual and spiritual synthesis of Mevlevîs and of all those who are interested in the *Mesnevî*. This conclusion seems even truer when one considers that out of ten partial commentaries, three only are edited, and only one is published, (and that in the twentieth century) from these commentaries of selected passages. This conclusion seems even truer when one considers that out of ten partial commentaries, three only are published, and only one is published from these commentaries of selected passages.

Of the five commentaries on Sineçak's work, only Cevrî's commentary was published (twice) in the nineteenth century. Cevrî, as we remember, is a disciple of Ankaravî; this seems to confirm the notion that Ankaravî's school of thought is the most official, and in a certain sense the most popular, among the Mevleviyya and beyond.

The commentary by Âbidin Paşa on the first eighteen verses of the *Mesnevî* is the only work of its sort to have been published. In this instance we must make another observation: Authors who lived at the time of the introduction and development of printing could propose their own works for publication, whereas in the case of the ancient authors publishers were faced with a choice as to whether their works should be considered classics.

The analysis of editorial choices made after the foundation of the Turkish Republic in 1923 must be adapted to a context which is completely changed. We have sometimes mentioned in a footnote whether a certain manuscript was published or not, or whether a certain work published before 1923 was ever re-issued in Latin characters, or even in a modern Turkish version. The choices made in these cases seem to favour works which were important for the maintenance of a certain Sufi Order tradition—one which was officially banned in 1925. That which has been defined as the 'Mevlevî phenomenon' in the final decades of the twentieth century and the first decade of the twenty-first, owing to a veritable infatuation with Mevlevî history and spirituality, has brought about an impressive number of publications and (a fact which is more important for the present inquiry) a goodly number of transcriptions into Latin characters of ancient works relating to the Mevleviye. That which printing failed to accomplish in the nineteenth century is finally beginning to be realised at the dawn of the twenty-first century.

Conclusion: The Ideal Library of the Dervish

On the basis of this all information, can we really speak of political choices regarding knowledge about Rûmî and his Sufi Order? Is it legitimate to speak of an ideal Mevlevî library? Certain observations can help the historian: anonymous works contained within compilations collections (*mecmua*) were very seldom printed during the nineteenth century. However, during the twentieth century and at the beginning of the twenty-first the printing of works of this sort becomes more and more common. After the great literary monuments come into print, then anonymous manuscripts have their turn (although many works still remain to be printed).

It is true that nineteenth century editors could not know the catalogues of manuscript libraries as well as those who lived during the twentieth century and the even more knowledgeable editors of today. Published material covers the entire gamut of the ideal (perhaps even ideological) Sufi Order construct: from hagiography to prayer book, passing via commentaries of the *Mesnevî* and via the history of the spiritual masters and *çelebis*. Even if this happened quite naturally, one cannot ignore the fact that printed works taken as a whole cover a goodly part of Mevlevî history. The more we move forward in the age of printing, the more we note that published works are written by contemporary authors. Consequently, some ancient works dating from early Mevlevî history have a hard time being published. Sahîh Ahmed Dede's work, for example, was published only recently, and only in the form of a transcription into Latin characters. Nineteenth Century writers, whether they are Mevlevî or not, have their books published even if their works are not as brilliant as those of the distant past. This may be normal: even today, critical editions of ancient texts are still lacking, whereas monographs on the same topics are published by many printing houses. Publishers generally select works of hagiography and books of devotions and show a bit less interest in historical texts. The translation, or the Ottoman Turkish version, of Eflâkî's book is always considered very important. Each author of ancient times considered it his duty to translate the official hagiography of the eponymous founder of the Mevlevî Order. This is an indication of the political choices made by these authors. However, at the time of the printing of these works, few Turkish translations are published.

If one were to write the history of Rûmî and his Sufi Order based only on works published in the nineteenth and twentieth centuries, one's knowledge would be considerable, without, nevertheless, being either exhaustive or perfect. Is it ultimately legitimate to speak of the Mevlevî Order having a specific policy, in and of itself? It is difficult to answer this question, unless one could prove that the Sufi Order was able to control or influence contemporary editors. One can, however, imagine that some Mevlevî authors might have been close to publishers or to people who worked with publishers, and used their personal influence—acting as an external consultants before the term was invented. It's certainly credible that people of this sort were influencing the concrete choices of publishers. The Mevlevîs themselves could have made their preferences known to publishers. Some work remains to be done, first to prove any correspondence between Mevlevîs and publishers, and second to undertake a precise study of the different publishers' catalogues. Nevertheless, the ideal library of the dervish, as it developed through the decades of the nineteenth century, has furnished an important base for the academic labours of the twenty-first century. We must remember that after the interdictions of 1925, interest in the printed works of the nineteenth century increased among the few people who could still read and understand Ottoman Turkish.

'This Sultan commands that my *Mesnevî* is a Master for all. By reading my *Mesnevî*, my disciple will become conscious of the problems of the twelve degrees of the divine names.'[48] Ankaravî's words on the role of the book (and even that of oral transmission and of the recitation of texts) in Mevlevî tradition, surely justify, for disciples of the Ottoman nineteenth century, the diffusion of printed works.

48. Fabio Ambrosio, 'Ecrire et décrire la confrérie Mevlevîyye entre le XVIe et XVIIe siècle ', in *Le soufisme à l'époque ottomane*, edited by Rachida Chih and Catherine Mayeur-Jaouen (Cairo: Institut Français d'archéologie orientale, 2010), 275–290.

Boundless Love: Ismā'īl al-Anqarawī's Commentary on the Preface to the Second Book of the *Mathnawī*

Immobile Passion in a Changing Context

The Forty Rules of Love,[1] the recent novel written by the famous Turkish novelist Elif Shafak, has renewed interest in an ancient theological passion, especially in Turkey. This novel concerns the divine passion, *'ishq* in Arabic, which corresponds to the divine *eros* in classical Greek. The story represents the life of a Rūmī completely changed after the meeting of the person who will be his friend, his spiritual master and finally his mirror, Shams al-Dīn Tabrīzī. While *The Forty Rules of Love* has inaugurated a new trend in the Turkish literature with a proliferation of novels inspired by the relationship between Rūmī and Shams,[2] at the same time the subject has stimulated anew the old doctrinal and theological debate about the meaning of love. Thus, it is quite common today, in any kind of bookshop throughout Turkey, to find new books by theologians or Sufi scholars about divine passion, or *'ishq*. In the last two years alone, more than one work has been published on the subject.[3]

1. Shafak Elif, *The Forty Rules of Love* (New York: Viking Penguin 2010) was first written in English although it appeared earlier in a Turkish version as Elif Şafak, *Aşk* (Istanbul: Doğan Yayıncılık 2009).
2. Among the many recent popular novels on this theme, we will cite one example: Yağmur Sinan, *Aşkın gözyaşları Şems-i Tebrizi: biyografik roman* (*The Lover's Tears, Shams of Tabriz: a Biographical Novel*) (Konya: Karatay Akademik Yayınları, 2010).
3. See for instance: Ahmet Arı, *Galib Dede'nin aşk ateşi: Şeyh Galib Divanı'nda aşk*, (Istanbul: Profil Yayıncılık 2008); Nusret Çam, *Aşk dini* (Istanbul: Ötüken Neşriyat 2010); İsmail Yakıt, *Mevlana'da aşk felsefesi* (Istanbul: Ötüken Neşriyat 2010); Metin Yasa, *Rubaileri ışığında Mevlana'da aşk ve işlevi* (Ankara: Elis Yayınları 2010); Yusuf Çetindağ, *Aşk üzerine*, (Istanbul: Kitabevi 2011).

Love being the key concept in the Sufi tradition, it should come as no surprise that most literary and philosophical writing about love in Islamic studies today seems to concentrate on love in the Sufi tradition. Sufism has promulgated the ideals, concepts and contemplative disciplines associated with love over the past 1200 years: that is, ever since the introduction of the term into the lexicon of Muslim mysticism thanks to Rābiʿa al-ʿAdawiyya (d 185/801).[4] Since her day, interest in love in mystical circles has never once abated.[5]

Long after the time of Rābiʿa, the thirteenth century experienced exactly the same debate. The nexus of literature, poetry and *Eros/ʿIshq* fascinated many Sufis of the period, and, of course, the passion for divine love was the ultimate preoccupation of the great master of Konya, Mawlānā Muḥammad Jalāl al-Dīn al-Balkhī al-Rūmī.[6] His

4. Geert Jan van Gelder, "Rābiʿa's Poem on the Two Kinds of Love: Mystification?" in *Verse and the Fair Sex. Studies in Arabic Poetry and in Representation of Women in Arabic Literature,* ed. Frederich de Jong, (Utrecht: M. T. Houtsma Strichting Publications 1993), pp. 66-76; Julian Baldick, "The Legend of Rabiʿa of Basra: Christian Antecedents, Muslim Counterparts," in *Religion*, 20 (1990), pp. 233-247; ʿAbd al-Raḥmān Badawī, *Shahīdat al-ʿishq al-ilāhī, Rābiʿa al-Adawiyya*, third edition (Cairo 1976); Margaret Smith, *Rabiʿa: The Life & Work of Rabiʿa and Other Women Mystics in Islam* (Oxford: Oneworld 1994).
5. Leonard Lewisohn, 'Romantic Love in Islam', in *Encyclopædia of Love in World Religions*, ed. Yudit Greenberg, (New York: Macmillan Reference & Thomson Gale 2007), volume II, 513–15; Ali b. Muhammad al-Daylami, *A Treatise on Mystical Love: Abū'l-Ḥasan ʿAlī b. Muḥammad al-Daylamī*, translated by JN Bell & HM Abdul Latif al Shafie (Edinburgh: Edinburgh University Press, 2005); Abū Ḥāmid al-Ghazālī, *L'Amore di Dio*; Italian translation by Carla Fabrizi, (Bologna: EMI 2004); Laury Silvers, '"God Loves Me": The Theological Content and Context of Early Pious and Sufi Women's Sayings on Love', in *Journal for Islamic Studies*, 30 (2010): 33–59; Maria Dakake, 'Guest of the Inmost Heart: Conceptions of the Divine Beloved among Early Sufi Women', in *Comparative Islamic Studies*, 3 (2007): 72–97; Binyamin Abrahamov, *Divine Love in Islamic Mysticism. The Teaching of al-Ghazālī and al-Dabbāgh* (London & New York: RoutledgeCurzon 2003).
6. For an introduction to the relationship between Rūmī and his Sufi order, see Alberto Fabio Ambrosio, *Dervisci: Storia, antropologia, mistica* (Roma: Carocci editore 2011); AF Ambrosio, E Pierunek, and Th Zarcone, *Les derviches tourneurs: doctrine, histoire et pratiques* (Paris: Les Editions du Cerf 2006); Leili Anvar Chenderoff, *Rūmī* (Paris: Editions Entrelacs 2004); Franklin D Lewis, *Rumi, Past and Present, East and West: The Life, Teaching and Poetry of Jalāl al-Dīn Rumi* (Oxford: Oneworld Publications 2000); William Chittick, *The Sufi Path of Love: The Spiritual Teachings of Rumi* (Albany: State University of New York Press, 1983); Abdülbâki Gölpınarlı, *Mevlânâ'dan sonra Mevlevilik* (Istanbul: İnkılâp ve Aka 1982).

poetry and his life story are pregnant with an inner tension and yearning for divine union. Any study of the thought and works of the spiritual ancestor of the Whirling Dervishes demands that one examine this fundamental topic. This is all the more true in that a widespread simplistic reading of the history of Sufi movements tends to oppose the philosophical school of Ibn 'Arabī (d 1240), based on knowledge, to the more emotional and ecstatic school represented by Rūmī himself, based on love.[7]

The present essay does not aspire to offer a general survey of the topic of love, but simply to provide an introduction to the treatment of the subject in the preface to Book II of Rūmī's *Mathnawī*, where he introduces the concept of love (*'ishq*), discusses its reality and definition, and implicitly reveals it to be the most important topic in his thought and work. Written partly in Persian and partly in Arabic, this preface is an interesting starting point for the present inquiry because in a few lines Rūmī opens up the debate, both spiritual and doctrinal, on the status of Love—or, more precisely, on the definition of the lover.

The essay will focus on the commentary by Ismā'īl Anqarawī (d 1041/1631) on the preface to the Book Two of the *Mathnawī*.[8] The interpretation of the text by Shaykh Anqarawī, who was known as the 'Grand Commentator on the *Mathnawī*' [*Şârih al-Mathnawī*] on the Rūmī's masterpiece,[9] belongs squarely within the living tradition of the Mevlevī Sufi Order and is especially significant since since he was

7. Omid Safi, 'Did the Two Oceans Meet? Connections and Disconnections between Ibn al-'Arabī and Rūmī', in *Journal of the Muhyiddin Ibn 'Arabi Society*, XXVI (1999): 55-88.

8. *Mathnawī-yi ma'nawī*, edited by RA Nicholson (Tehran: Amīr Kabīr 1357A. Hsh./1976). In the present article we refer to the recent annotated verse translation by Jawid Mojaddedi: *The Masnavi: Book Two*, (Oxford: Oxford University Press 2007). For a more traditional translation, also very important for the study of Rumi in the West, see RA Nicholson, *The Mathnawí of Jalálu'ddín Rúmi, edited with critical notes, translation, and commentary*, edited by RA Nicholson, 8 volumes (London: Luzac, 1925–1940).

9. Alberto Fabio Ambrosio, *Vie d'un Derviche Tourneur: doctrine et rituels du soufisme au XVIIe siècle*, (Paris: CNRS Editions 2010); Alberto Fabio Ambrosio, 'Galata Mevlevihanesi'nde Şeyh Olmak/Being a Shaykh in Galata', in *Saltanatın Dervişleri Dervişlerin Saltanatı İstanbul'da Mevlevilik/The Dervishes of Sovereignty, the Sovereignty of Dervishes: the Mevlevi Order in Istanbul* (Istanbul: Istanbul Araştırmalar Enstitüsü 2007), 42–56.

considered the grand spiritual master for later generations of Mevlevī dervishes. Anqarawī's works offers both a very deep interpretation of Rūmī's thought and a highly organized presentation of Mevlevī spiritual practices.

Three and a half centuries after Mawlānā Rūmī's death, Anqarawī had to spend much time and energy defending the Order against violent attacks on Sufi rituals as well as on other Sufis, particularly the Khalwatiyya, by members of a powerful religious movement of preachers known as 'Kadizâdelîs'. Their doctrine was highly hostile towards the Sufis, whose practices they viewed as a degeneration of the true Islamic religion. This religious decadence *avant la lettre* was, to their mind, the reason behind the social and political decline of the Ottoman Empire. The empire appeared to them to be in trouble regarding its notoriously ambitious foreign policy—which was not the objective and historical reality of the situation, for which the Kadizâdelîs blamed the Sufis with their strange practices of corrupting the religion of the Prophet. The Sufis were not alone in being the butt of criticism and the attacks by this puritanical—as some Turkish scholars have described it—religious sect, whose preachers also assailed a number of common religious practices, sometimes classified as 'popular' or 'superstitious', such as visiting the tombs of saints, the *awliyā* or friends of God. From the thirteenth to the seventeenth century, from Rūmī's to Anqarawī's time, the social situation of the Sufis seems to have been changed, but their doctrines had withstood the test of time, remaining, in a certain way, not only unmodified in respect to principles but, theosophically speaking, becoming more elaborate, refined and profound.[10]

The approach adopted in this essay is both historical and philosophical, aiming to attain a deeper understanding of what is called the 'Religion of Love' in the Rūmī's thought through an

10. Alberto Fabio Ambrosio, 'İsmā'īl Rusūhī Anqarawī: An Early Mevlevi Intervention into the Emerging Kadızadeli-Sufi Conflict', in J Curry and E Ohlander, editors, *Sufism and Society: Arrangements of the Mystical in the Muslim World, 1200–1800* (London: Routledge 2011), 183–97; Alberto Fabio Ambrosio, 'Ecrire et décrire la confrérie Mevleviyye entre le XVIe et XVIIe siècle', in *Le Soufisme à l'époque ottomane XVe—XVIIIe siècle*, edited by R Chih, C Mayeur-Jaouen, D Gril, and R McGregor, (Cairo: IFAO 2010), 275–90; Madeline C Zilfi, *The Politics of Piety: the Ottoman Ulema in the Postclassical Age (1600–1800)* (Minneapolis: Bibliotheca Islamica 1988).

analysis of Anqarawī's commentary as well as an exploration of the historical development of Rumi's doctrine of *eros*. It is not common to find the analysis of the development of a doctrine situated in a context of changing social and political influences. The debate between philosophy-oriented essentialists and historicists centres on comparison of texts from different periods and changes in religious practice. As well as enabling us to explore Rūmī's thought and its development in the Mevlevī tradition, this specific topic may also provide keys for understanding spiritual life from a more universal perspective.

From Text to Philosophy

According to the method of the rhetorical analysis devised, in the case of Rūmī's *Mathnawī*, by Safavi and Weightman, the introduction to the second book of the *Mathnawī* represents also a good example of a complex literary design and texture.[11] This preface is dense in philosophy and doctrine, and may perhaps be described as a manifesto of Sufi ideals rather than just a simple introduction. Rūmī seems to stress at least three concepts of importance for a correct understanding of the subtle topic of *'ishq:* the slave, the lover and the limit. But why these *three* concepts and whence this tripartite division? The text itself seems to be conceived in three parts, of which the first and the last constitute a special figure of speech called 'rhetorical inclusion'. Rūmī, starting his second *daftar*, uses a literary pretext, even if, albeit, it may be historically true:

> Here is the reason for the postponement of this second volume: if all divine wisdom should be made known to the slave [of God] at once, the benefits in it would leave him unable to act, and the infinite wisdom of God would obliterate his comprehension. He would not be able to cope.[12]

The stress here is on the action of the slave. Who is this slave? Is he Rūmī himself? Perhaps. But the slave may also represent mankind in search of divine wisdom. Is the slave the true Sufi? The answer seems to be given by the author himself in the last paragraph of the Introduction:

11. Seyed Gharreman Safavi and Simon Weightman, *Rūmī's Mystical Design: Reading the* Mathnawī, *Book One* (Albany: SUNY 2009).
12. Translated by Mojaddedi, *The Masnavi: Book Two*, 3.

> Someone asked, 'What is a lover?' I answered, 'You will know when you become like us.' True love cannot be measured, which is why it is said to be an attribute of God in reality, and applicable to the slave only metaphorically. 'He loves them'– this is the totality; 'and they love Him'—do 'they' exist though in reality?.[13]

It is probable that Rūmī here provides an answer to his own reflections about the status of the slave. Who then is this slave? He is the lover to whom divine Love applies in a metaphorical way. The first and last parts of the Introduction are general statements of the simple truth that an orientation towards an answer may itself represent an answer. The middle section of the text, however, investigates a far deeper Sufi interpretation. This longer paragraph forms a transition between the introduction and conclusion, providing a logical passage from one to another. Let's listen to the Sufi logic of Rūmī:

> This is why God makes a little of that infinite wisdom into a toggle which can be put into his nostrils, to lead him like a camel towards the necessary action. If He were not to inform him of those benefits, he would not move at all, because knowledge of the gain to be made is what motivates human beings, who say, 'For the sake of this I will do what is right.' If He should pour infinite wisdom down on him, the slave would be unable to move, just as a camel will not walk unless a toggle is put into its nose of an appropriate size—if the toggle is too big it will just slump down: 'There is nothing, the storehouse of which is not with Us. And We only send it down in a fixed measure.'[14] Without water, clay cannot be made into a brick, nor can it become a brick if the water is excessive. 'He has raised the sky and He has set up the scales.'[15]

This paragraph seems to affirm the idea of moderation in God's offering His benefits to human beings. There is divine *rationale* and *ratio* underlying these benefits. Here, the Latin word *ratio* means a

13. Translated by Mojaddedi, *The Masnavi: Book Two,* 3. The reference is to: 'O you who believe, whoever amongst you becomes a renegade from his religion, know that in his stead God will bring a people whom He loves and who love Him…' (Qur'ān V: 54).
14. Qur'ān, XV: 21
15. The reference is to Qur'ān, LV: 7

number or measure, that is, the right number and true proportion prevailing throughout every relation existing in the world. God's rationale, His *ratio,* thus consists in His providing everyone what he needs according to his own particular circumstances. Divine Justice is attentive to the capacity of the receiver, who is not able to receive the entire infinite wisdom, but only that which he requires and has the aptitude to absorb.[16] Such moderation, *ratio* and balance pertains to God's wisdom, a doctrine that also appears throughout the Qur'ān (XV: 21; LV: 7) which teaches that there is a certain wisdom and measure underlying the blessings and benefits bestowed by God. In Rūmī's text here one thus finds the association of wisdom with the idea of balance, equilibrium and moderation. There is little space here for what is limitless and infinite; the paragraph suggests the notion of a *ratio* as a limited field and the idea of *reason* (in Arabic and Persian, *'aql*) as a fetter, bond and measured limit.[17]

One may ask, what kind of philosophical or doctrinal principle it might be that could disturb the principle of the moderation of wisdom that appears to be so fundamental in the Introduction of the Second Book of the *Mathnawī*? The answer—and the crucial turning point—appears in the next sentence, where Rūmī once again supports his message with a verse from the Qur'ān:

> He gives everything in the right proportion, not without measurement and calculation, apart from to those people who have been transformed from their physical forms, becoming the ones referred to when He says, 'He provides without calculation for whomsoever He chooses.'"[18]

16. Rūmī's way of thinking here reflects certain aspects of medieval scholastic thought, recalling the *adage* that: 'all that is received is received according to its own capacity of receptivity' (*quidquid recipitur ad modum recipientis recipitur*). See Thomas Aquinas, *Summa Theologiae*, I Q. 75 a. 5.
17. "The word *'aql* itself means etymologically that which binds or limits. From the perspective of Islam, it keeps man on the Straight Path of faith and binds him to its truth. Numerous verses in the Quran describe those who go astray and reject faith as people who do not use their intellect or mind, *'aql,* (one recalls phrases such as *lā ya'qilūn*, "they do not understand" or literally "do not use their minds," and *la yafqahūn*, "they do not comprehend"). It is this intellect or mind that responds to faith and constitutes the instrument through which knowledge of God is obtained. In the language of the Quran, *'aql* is at once both intellect and reason." Omaima Abou-Bakr, 'Abrogation of the Mind in the Poetry of Jalal al-Din Rumi', in *Alif: Journal of Comparative Poetics*, 14 (1994): 37–63, 46.
18. *The Masnavi: Book Two*, translated by Mojaddedi, 3. Qur'ān, V: 212.

Everything is given by God in exactly the right proportion and amount, according to a measurement and calculation that is precisely assessed. Yet at this point, Rūmī switches his statement, changes his perspective, and, using a negative sentence to affirm a positive meaning, takes exception to the general rule of moderation broached above. Rūmī's Introduction changes direction here, to describe an exceptional category of people: advanced mystics who have been transformed beyond the normal creaturely state of being. For such elect adepts, God provides His blessings *without any measure or calculation*. By divine election and the power of God's Will, because He has chosen them, these mystics are the ones who can escape from the law of moderation. To them the bondage of the *rational* and *ratio* does not apply. The divine Will Itself overrides the moderation of God's wisdom. The principle that disturbs the equilibrium is thus the very Will of God which chooses those whom He loves. What is reasonable, rational and measured contains an aspect of limitation as well as the idea of intention, for all that is reasonable has its own limit and intent. But those who have been chosen and transformed by the will of God realise that which is boundless, without *ratio* or limitation.

The lover, animated by God's Will, enjoys that experience without any limits which is love. The lover reaches a position where the limit is crossed, where the *ratio* and measure is not anymore what is ultimately intended. Rūmī finishes his reflection with this remark: 'Whoever hasn't tasted will not yet be aware'.[19] The lover's experience is a 'taste' rather than a 'measure', being beyond all rational limits and proportions. Reason here is abrogated and gives way to a love grounded in the Will of God.

Exactly the same conclusion has been reached in a recent study of Rumi's mystical poetry. The poems of Rūmī not only constitute a very remarkable literary achievement, but also represent a special experience of the 'abrogation of the mind', as Omaima Abou-Bakr has asserted:

> The exuberance, profuseness, and lack of organized thought are essential qualities of the persona's visionary madness. Poems may appear disjointed in form only because they are organized according to a scheme of visionary logic, or rather

19. *The Masnavi: Book Two*, translated by Mojaddedi, 3.

> illogic. The display of changing pictures or tableaux and the shifts of voice reveal the texture of an intoxicated state, at odds with systematic deduction. We should not require conventional cogency or coherence because the poet's interest is otherwise. The poetry, in its language and imagery, enacts the very 'madness' it conveys in the persona and his mystical experience. And it is for the reader to grasp the higher wisdom behind this 'madness'.[20]

As we have seen, Rūmī begins the second book of the *Mathnawī* with an excursus on the doctrine of God's measuring out His blessings as benefits His wisdom. Yet how did the Mevlevī tradition comment on this inspiring text? Did it represent a starting point for any particular Mevlevī philosophy of Providence? Reading this text, can we advance any new conclusions regarding the rhetorical analysis of the *Mathnawī*? To answer these and other questions, let us take a look at the commentary by Anqarawī, the grand Sufi commentator on the *Mathnawī,* to see what kind of Mevlevī philosophy he found within this Introduction.

Reason and Love in Anqarawī's Commentary: Excursus on the Limitations of Reason

Rhetorical analysis of the text of the *Mathnawī* has led to conclusions that seem to be supported by the Mevlevī exegetical tradition, in which Anqarawī is a major authority. In fact, "the Shaykh of Galata" (a district on the European side of Istanbul, where Anqarawī lived) commented on every verse of the entire *Mathnawī,* having been influenced by the Ottoman tradition associated with the school of Ibn 'Arabī.[21]

First of all, Anqarawī states that 'it is related that for nearly one or two years after having completed the writing of the first volume, the great master (in Turkish, *Hüdavendigar*) did not write anything at all. Then, some of the reasons for the delay and divine wisdom behind it

20. Omaima Abou-Bakr, 'Abrogation of the Mind in the Poetry of Jalal al-Din Rumi', 53.
21. Semih Ceyhan, *İsmail Ankaravî ve Mesnevî Şerhi*, PhD Thesis Bursa: T. C. Uludağ Üniversitesi Sosyal Bilimler Enstitüsü Temel İslam Bilimleri Anabilim Dalı Tasavvuf Bilim Dali, 2005. This dissertation is an excellent reference for comprehension of the Anqarawī's method of commentary on the *Mathnawī.*

became manifest to his enlightened inner being.'[22] By this statement, Anqarawī seems to affirm that from the completion of the first book to the inspiration of the second book of the *Mathnawī*, Rumi had to wait a quite long time for reasons of divine providence. But finally, the Galata Shaykh writes, Rumi summed up the divine wisdom behind this delay in poetic inspiration in his Introduction (*dîbâçe*).

Commenting on the middle part of the text, analysed above, the Grand Commentator repeats that order and moderation in the granting of divine benefits are the basis of all justice. In fact, Anqarawī also interprets the discourse of his master in terms of divine justice, noting that 'in every thing there is a necessity for justice (*'adalet*). If equilibrium (*tesviye*) and justice (*'adalet*) were not there, there would be no order (*intizâm*) in existence.'[23] A few lines later, he clarifies this statement by adding that that "that this is so every reality (*her hakk*) may reach exactly what it rightly deserves and every thing realise what suits its capacity, so that all the affairs of the world be organized harmoniously, and the circumstances of all things be directed aright.[24]

Anqarawī then develops the idea of justice in the realm of wisdom. In fact, the wisdom depicted up until now is more on the order of theodicy rather than the simple reason underlying everything. As mentioned above, it is *ratio* that supports justice, the two being intimately linked. Justice, especially divine Justice, oversees and directs all existence. For that reason, Anqarawī discards the use of the term *hakk* (truth, reality), which can also refer to divine Reality or the Reality of God Himself, instead affirming that everything must attain its own capacity within the limits of *reason.* All being seems to be embodied within reasonable limits or the limitations of reason: in other words, reason itself is the limit under the guidance of divine Wisdom. Anqarawī continues by affirming that: 'God Most High never vouchsafes anything to anyone without exact measure,

22. İsmail Rüsûhî Ankaravî, *Mecmûatü'l-Letâif ve Metmûratü'l Maarif (Şerhü'l-Mesnevî)*, volume 7, (Istanbul: Matbaa-i Âmire, 1289/1872), volume 1, 3. See also the Persian translation by 'Iṣmat Sattārzādah: *Sharḥ-i kabīr-i Anqarawī bar Mathnawī-yi Mawlawī*, 15 volumes (Tehran: Zarrīn 1374 A.Hsh./1995; reprinted several times). The passages discussed below are in volume 4, 2–6.
23. Ankaravî, *Mecmûatü'l-Letâif*, volume I, 4; *Sharḥ-i kabīr-i Anqarawī*, translated by Sattārzādah, volume 4, 3.
24. *Sharḥ-i kabīr-i Anqarawī*, translated by Sattārzādah, volume 4, 3.

accounting and balance; nothing is ever granted which is outside the demands of intelligence (*akl*)'.[25]

Here the Shaykh of Galata introduces a key word—intelligence (*akl*)—that is not found in Rumi's own text. The 'reason' by which divine Wisdom oversees everything is precisely the intelligence (or in the language of medieval philosophy, the *intellectus*). The divine *intellectus* determines and orders everything within the limits of the reason. Yet something escapes the dictates of this law, which leads Anqarawī to ask, 'After having said that nothing is ever vouchsafed to anyone except according to exact measure (*hesap*) and balance, a question arises, namely: "Are the saints (*evliya*) and the prophets (*enbiya*) in the same case as everyone else?"'.[26]

While Rūmī leaves this question unanswered, Anqarawī immediately states that there is a category of people who transcend this law, evading reasonable limits and escaping the limitations of reason. 'Save for this group' he adds, 'nothing is ever given without measure. Those vouchsafed [divine blessings] without measure are those who have been transformed from [i.e. made to transcend] the degree of creaturehood and ordinary humanity . . . such persons exemplify God's devotees'.[27] Thus it is that the saints and the prophets can transcend the limits of reason by being immersed in the divine Will. Then, commenting on the last sentence, Anqarawī, using specifically the terminology of Sufism, further expounds this notion:

> '*Whoever hasn't tasted will not yet be aware.*' [That is to say] 'Whoever hasn't tasted this secret (*sirr*) cannot know, insofar as any human being has not yet realized this degree (*mertebe*) cannot have any understanding of the states of its adepts. For even if the exoteric doctors of Law ('*ulemâ*) may have some theoretical knowledge of it, their knowledge is not personally experiential or interiorized.'[28]

The Shaykh of Galata explains that it is impossible to understand the interior mystery of Sufi doctrine without first personally 'tasting'

25. Ankaravî, *Mecmûatü'l-Letâif*, volume I, 4; *Sharḥ-i kabīr-i Anqarawī*, trans. Sattārzādah, volume 4, 4.
26. *Sharḥ-i kabīr-i Anqarawī*, trans. Sattārzādah, volume 4, 4.
27. *Sharḥ-i kabīr-i Anqarawī*, trans. Sattārzādah, volume 4, 4.
28. *Sharḥ-i kabīr-i Anqarawī*, trans. Sattārzādah, volume 4, 4.

or experiencing it. Attaining a spiritual level means becoming the 'master' of its state, an adept in that condition. The challenge of the experience of spiritual states is represented by the religious or mystical secret that is the ultimate goal of the Sufi Path. The 'taste' of the Sufi's life is also its secret.

At this point Anqarawī delves even deeper into reading the text of his master, further developing and elaborating certain esoteric elements in the Introduction.

The Heart has Reasons which Reason Knows Not

Anqarawī commentary on the next passage refers to the state of the true lover:

> Someone asked, 'What is a lover?' I answered, 'You will know when you become like us.'

The debate concerns the relationship between 'passionate love' (*'ishq*) and *maḥabbat,* the latter being love as a simple feeling of affection, more or less equivalent to the Greek term *agape*. The meanings of both these terms here are extremely important, because translating them into Western philosophical and theological terms influenced by Christian doctrine sometimes conveys connotations that completely misrepresent their Arabic originals.

In Rūmī's text this passage occurs unexpectedly, the transition from the preceding text being very abrupt. In his commentary however, Anqarawī approaches Rūmī's text more like a philosopher, translating the words of his master in a theoretical way, turning his sudden poetic utterances into elements of an intellectual debate. Whereas the question set down in Rūmī's Introduction was simply 'What is a lover?' in Anqarawī's translation, this question is interpreted as being a special request to Rūmī himself: 'Someone asked me: O Mawlānā, what is the state of the lover (*aşıklık*)?'[29] In the next sentence, Anqarawī's interpretation exposes his doctrinal orientation:

> Love (*aşk*) and affection (*muhabbet*) have no end (*nihayet*) or measure (*hesap*). (In some manuscripts, between the words for 'love' and 'affection', the conjunction "and" is not found.

29. *Sharḥ-i kabīr-i Anqarawī*, trans. Sattārzādah, volume 4, 4.

> According to this [latter] reading, the meaning of the term *aşk* (love) would be *muhabbet* (friendship) without limit or measure.[30]

Anqarawī states that in certain manuscripts of the *Mathnawī* one finds the word *'ishq* (love) instead of *'āshiq* (lover), implying that the question posed concerns the status of love more than that of the lover. For this reason, after the above-cited question about the identity of the lover, Rūmī gives an answer focused on the meaning of love, explaining that 'True love cannot be measured, which is why it is said to be an attribute of God in reality and applicable to the slave only metaphorically.'[31]

Anqarawī comments on this statement as follows: 'The reason why Rūmī states that love (*'ishq*) and friendship (*maḥabbat*) 'are an attribute of God in reality' is because love and friendship have no limit (*nihāya*) just as with this attribute of God Almighty; the attributes of God are likewise infinitely limitless.'[32] Elaborating on the merely metaphorical attribution of love to man, Anqarawī explains that love is without measure because it depends on God's attribute of boundless love. Love is essentially divine, a quality belonging to God. In respect to the human being, the 'slave', love is different because infinite and limitless love can only be attributed to man in a metaphorical way:

> The attribution of love (*muhabbet*) to the slave is but metaphorical, a mere figure of speech (*majāz*), because in reality affection (*muhabbet*) belongs to God (*Hakk*) alone, just as [according to the Sacred Tradition]: 'I was a hidden treasure and I loved to be known.'[33] Love (*muhabbet*) is an eternal attribute of God (*Hakk*).[34]

30. *Sharḥ-i kabīr-i Anqarawī*, trans. Sattārzādah, volume 4, 4.
31. *The Masnavi: Book Two*, translated by Mojaddedi, 3.
32. Ankaravî, *Mecmûatü'l-Letâif*, volume I, 4; *Sharḥ-i kabīr-i Anqarawī*, translated by Sattārzādah, volume 4, 4.
33. On this *ḥadīth*, see Badi' al-Zamān Furūzānfar, *Aḥādīth-i Mathnawī* (Tehran: Dānishgāh-i Tihrān, 1335 sh./1956; reprinted Amīr Kabīr 1361 A.Hsh./1982), 29, no 70. *CF* Ibn 'Arabi, *al-Futūḥāt al-Makkiyya* (Cairo, 1911), volume II, 322; *Mathnawī*, II: 364; Dârimî, *Sunan*, I/17 in Yardım, Ali, *Mesnevî hadisleri (Tesbît ve Tahrîc)* (Istanbul: Damla Yayınevi 2008), 93–94.
34. Ankaravî, *Mecmûatü'l-Letâif*, volume I, 4; *Sharḥ-i kabīr-i Anqarawī*, trans. Sattārzādah, volume 4, 4.

Anqarawī uses the adjective 'eternal' (*qadīm*) here to explain that love in respect to God is boundless, stressing that in accordance with the eternity of the Divinity, love is without limit, God Himself being without limit or reason (*ratio*). However, loving-kindness, love-as-friendship (*muhabbet*) or *agape* essentially characterizes the lover. A lover is one who enjoys a special experience by way of 'tasting' love without any moderation; he is one who plunges into the ocean of this spiritual state.

Genitival Love

We now come to the final passage in Rūmī's Introduction cited above: "'He loves them'—this is the totality; 'and they love Him'—do 'they' exist though in reality?"[35] It would seem that the question posed here acts as a kind of grammatical genitive of Love, in the sense that love is always the love of someone for someone else: the love of God for the slave or the love of the slave for God, even if, in the latter case, that would be merely a metaphorical way of speaking. In addition, love seems to belong to the category of the manifestation of an inner state.

Love always seems to be the love of somebody for someone or something for its object; the lover aspiring to reach the object of his longing. All medieval philosophy taught the truth that the first action of the will is to attain the goal of its own desire. Love, in this fashion can be correctly seen as being the primordial, first action of the will. Because God is the Supreme Being, He must also have this essential attribute. Anqarawī elaborates this way of thinking about the divine attribute of love as follows:

> 'He loves them' means that God Almighty loves the believers, in which respect His word is complete (*tamām*) and final (*kāfiya*). He is the Reality [of everything] and their primordial origin. 'And they love Him' means that the believers love God only insofar as love in essence originates in God's relationship to his slaves [humankind]; it is God's love that later causes love to become manifest in them [human beings]. Since God out of the immensity of His Essence has already manifested love towards his slaves, it would be impossible for the slave of God [of his own accord] to manifest love (*muhabbet eder*)

35. *The Masnavi: Book Two*, translated by Mojaddedi, 3.

> for God, nor would he have the capacity to do so. Therefore, the love (*muhabbet*) that the slave has for God is merely of a metaphorical and nominal nature (*'itibarī*).[36]

This really brilliant passage can considered as a short treatise on the meaning of divine love—understood both as the love of God for the slave and as the love of the slave for God. Anqarawī reflects that the Love of God is the beginning and the end of everything, comprising the primordial element underlying every form of love in creatures. The human person's love is a manifestation of God's love and thus the love of God within a person ('the slave') can only be understood as having metaphorical significance because the attribute of love ultimately belongs to God alone. In reality, the human only loves because God loves, for only by God's will does the human being or, more precisely the believer, manifest love.[37]

From this point onwards, Anqarawī sets Rūmī's text to one side and directs his attention to commenting on this Qur'ānic verse cited by Rūmī:

> O you who believe! Whoso of you becomes a renegade from his religion, know that in his stead, God will bring a people who He loves and who love Him, humble toward believers, stern toward disbelievers, striving in the way of God, and fearing not the blame of any blamer. (V: 54)

Focusing on the divinely revealed scripture, he directs his interpretation toward a more precise meaning of the verse under debate:

> 'By referring to those who were later to fall into the sin of apostasy, this verse of the Qur'ān testifies to the occult divine decree that underpinned an historical event before it actually came to pass. In sum, this passage of the Scripture refers to an event that occurred after the death of the Prophet (be peace upon him!), when a number of groups who had previously converted to Islam, such as al-Musaylima the Liar

36. Ankaravî, *Mecmûatü'l-Letâif*, volume I, 4–5; *Sharḥ-i kabīr-i Anqarawī*, translated by Sattārzādah, volume 4, 5.

37. This doctrine is found throughout Rumi's *Mathnawī*. See, for example, book I: 1784–89.

> (al-Kadhāb) and Talayḥat ibn Khwayald, who belonged to the Banī Asad [Quraysh] tribe, became apostates. A number of other groups joined their ranks and turned apostates [against the Prophet Muḥammad] and professed the prophethood of Musaylima the Liar[38] and Ṭalha ibn Khawayald. Referring to these apostates, God Almighty informs us that anyone who renounces his faith and becomes an apostate, after first condemning them to perdition, He will then bring another people into existence "who He loves and who love Him.' Although referring to these local Arabs in this phrase, God Almighty also signifies the entire nation of the Arabs.[39]

Here the Grand Commentator broaches the subject of the love of God in the Qur'ān, stressing the need to put it in correct historical context. Anqarawī's interpretation of this scriptural passage, however, concerns far more than the love of God. He teaches that God's love is directed toward a people who turn towards Him, who convert to following the true religion. Gathering together into one nation the true believers, God loves them and they love Him. God's love comes to them after their conversion to the true religion and the one true God. Here, we are faced with a traditional exoteric Islamic commentary and interpretation of the meaning of the love of God, in which the Qur'ān's text is given pride of place and Anqarawī's reasoning and interpretation of the divinely revealed word of God is presented in an entirely legalistic and orthodox fashion. Anqarawī next proceeds to discuss the meaning of 'love' (*maḥabbat*) according to the understanding of the exoteric theologians:

> There are a good number of opinions pronounced by doctors of the Law (*'ulemâ*) about the phrase 'who He loves and who love Him'. The exoteric doctors of the Law (*'ulemâ-i zahir*), along with some of the scholastic theologians (*mutakkilīm*), believed that 'love (*muhabbet*) is the inclination of the soul toward perfect apprehension of the object of love.' They have also stated that love is a kind of will (*irâdet*) and the attachment

38. Maslama (or Musaylima, a diminutive used as a term of contempt for him by Muslims) was a rival prophet to Muḥammad, whose revolt was crushed in 12/633 by an army led by Khālid ibn Walīd.
39. Ankaravî, *Mecmûatü'l-Letâif*, volume I, 5; *Sharḥ-i kabīr-i Anqarawī*, trans. Sattārzādah, volume 4, 5.

> of the will [to a love object] due to certain circumstances or due to the beneficence (*ihsân*) experienced [from the love object], thus prompting [one to perform] service and obedience for the sake of benefits found through love. It would be impossible to love God's Essence or Attributes if love was anything else but this. They also profess that man's ('the slave's') love of God is a love for God's boons (*an'âm*) and beneficence, and that man's service and obedience [of God] expresses man's love of God's mercy. However, God's love for man ('the slave') is merely the divine remittance of goodness and beneficence to him.
>
> But according to the mystics who have experientially personally realized the truth (*muḥaqiqīn*), the above opinion [about love] is considered weak since as these realized adepts (*arbāb-i taḥqīq*) understand it, God's love is eternal and man's love merely temporal. For these reasons, they [the Sufi mystics] state that 'the devotee's love for God is the annihilation of the condition of humanity through the eternal subsistence of the Divinity, whereas God's love towards the devotee is the eternal subsistence of the Divinity through the annihilation of the condition of humanity.'[40]

Here we see how the debate has been nonchalantly switched from a discussion of the status of the lover (*'âshiqlik*) to an analysis of the notion of love, all the while using the Arabic abstract verbal noun: *maḥabbat*. In the final paragraph, it is interesting that Anqarawī doesn't mention either the term or reality of *'ishq* (passionate love) which was the beginning point and original inspiration behind Rūmī's text. The problem appears to be that the term *'ishq* is non-Qur'ānic and thus is more problematic to use than *maḥabbat* in a traditional religious context to interpret the meaning of love. As a matter of fact, the transition from the term *'ishq* to *maḥabbat* is not very long, even if it imposes a change of perspective. The notion of *'ishq* implies a movement of intense passion, expressive of a strong tension that is often absent from the term *maḥabbat*. *Maḥabbat* in

40. Ankaravî, *Mecmûatü'l-Letâif*, volume I, 5; *Sharḥ-i kabīr-i Anqarawī*, translated by Sattārzādah, volume 4, 5–6. The Arabic of the above passage is: *Fiān maḥabbat al-'abd-Allah āfnā' al-nāsūtiya fī baqā' al-lahūtiya wa maḥabbat Allāh li'l-'abd abqā' al-lahūtiya fī fanā' al-nāsūtiya.*

this short passage, on the other hand, is conceived of as harbouring a religious tension, being connected to virtue, service and obedience to God. Nevertheless, between the lines, the commentary betrays a sense that the term *maḥabbat* is perhaps too weak a term to convey any real experience of union.

At the conclusion of his commentary on Rumi's Introduction, Anqarawī returns to the notion of intelligence or *intellectus* mentioned above, combining his theory of love with speculation on contemplative vision:

> If one were to contemplate with the innermost conscience and regard [the issue of love] with the eye of interior vision, neither lover nor beloved but the divine Reality can be said to exist throughout all the multiple levels [of existence], as in the verse:
>
> That passage, 'Who He loves and who love Him'—what does it really mean?
> For He's both Shopper and the Shop—is it not all just masquerade?
>
> In a word, there are so many issues involved in the subject of love that no proper treatment of the matter can be fit in this brief disquisition.[41]

As can be seen from this passage, love and the Beloved represent the final goal of contemplation during every spiritual state experienced by the believer. If man loves God, he can only contemplate God-the-Beloved thanks to the God Himself, that is, thanks to *amor divino*. At the end of the mystical journey (*sayr u sulūk—seyr-i sülūk*), from the standpoint of the interior contemplative vision, only the experience of love and the Beloved remains. To continue talking about love here is meaningless since the word appears devoid of reality.

The Fire of Love

The Qur'ānic verse excerpted from the Sura Maida (V: 54) is also commented on by Anqarawī in his commentary on the Poem of Sufi

41. Ankaravî, *Mecmûatü'l-Letâif*, volume I, 5; *Sharḥ-i kabīr-i Anqarawī*, trans. Sattārzādah, volume 4, 6.

Way, or the Ode in T Major (*Tā'iyah*) by Ibn al-Fāriḍ (d 632/1235).[42] Expounding the twelfth and particularly the thirteenth verses on this poem, Anqarawī reflects once more on the meanings of *'ishq* and *maḥabbat*. Here are Ibn Fâriḍ's verses in question:

> A passion betrayed
> by telling tears;
> a grief inflamed by burning pains
> consuming me with their disease.
>
> Noah's flood is like
> my wailing tears,
> Abraham's blazing fire like
> my pangs of love.[43]

Let us listen to Anqarawī's commentary on the second verse ('Noah's flood . . .'):

> As exaggerated as it can appear the situation depicted in these verses is nevertheless true. On the one hand, the fire of Abraham is corporeal and consequently finite, while on the other the fire of the love (*muhabbet*) is spiritual and eternal. The spiritual pleasure and liberation experienced is just as strong and delightful as the corporeal pleasure, and the spiritual anguish and afflictions that ensue from them are naturally violent and troublesome. An explanation of the situation is as follows: In reality, love (*muhabbet*) is an attribute of the Divinity (*Hakk*) according to the statements, 'I loved to be known'[44] and 'Who He loves and who love Him' (Qur'ān, V: 54). From this point of view, love (*muhabbet*) is one of the most primordial attributes of the Divinity and although other things are finite in relation to the attributes of God, love is not finite. So divine Love in appearing in the lover reveals Its own works. For example, the sense of love is so hot

42. *'Umar Ibn al-Fāriḍ: Sufi Verse, Saintly Life*, trans. Th Emil Homerin, (New York: Paulist Press 2001), 73–291.
43. *'Umar Ibn al-Fāriḍ. Sufi Verse, Saintly Life*, 77.
44. A reference to the Ḥadīth: 'I was a hidden treasure and I loved to be known so I created the world'—mentioned in Badi' al-Zamān Furūzānfar, *Aḥādīth-i Mathnawī* (Tehran: Danishgah-i Tihran, 1335 A.Hsh./1956; reprinted Amīr Kabīr 1361 A.Hsh./1982), no 70.

> and intense that he cannot separate it from himself so that the lover doesn't have the power to relinquish the Beloved. Such love sometimes reveals its effects which are derived from the lover's hope of meeting the Beloved, in which case, enthusiasm, freshness and joy are necessarily manifested [in the lover]. Sometimes, due to the fear of being deprived [of the Beloved] and the anguish of the separation, the fire of love (*muhabbet*) causes the lover to experience a certain hardening and rigidity, so that he becomes drowned in grief and sorrow. When this happens and the lover falls into a state of sorrow and grief, because of the strength of his sadness and the force of destiny, his body becomes weak and he falls into a state of miserable poverty. When the fire of love and the obduracy of the sadness he experiences become more and more violent, an interior burning occurs and the inner steam grows more and more oppressive. If this steam mounts up, tears are shed; he begins to weep, his cries full of wailing and lamentation. So tears begin to flow out from the corners of his weepy eyes and as the steam mounts up to his head, it is called a flowing stream (*'abera*) of tears.[45]

After having read this moving passage that is so expressive of the sorrow of love, the sensitive reader might feel the need to cry. Anqarawī, of course, is commenting on a deep Sufi poem whose language is very dense. His commentary here is also different from his exegesis on the *Mathnawī* where he was compelled to explain the subject-matter in greater detail to his disciples. In this passage, Anqarawī also shows the coherence of his thought. Love (*muhabbet*) is such a strong feeling that it can cause the body of the believer/lover to tremble and shake with passion. This passion is not merely contemplative but active; it requires the observance of good manners in serving God in addition to the deep feelings of nostalgia that the soul feels, longing to return to its divine Origin.

In another of his works, *The Pilgrims' Path* (*Minhâc'ül-fukarâ*), Anqarawī also discusses the meaning of love. Following 'Abdu'llāh Anṣārī's (d 481/1089) categorisation, he states clearly that *muhabbet* is either a mystical state (*hâl*) or a spiritual station (*makâm*). Translating

45. İsmail Rusûhî Ankaravî, *Osmanlı Tasavvuf Düşüncesi—İbn'ül-Fârız'ın Kasîde-i Tâiyye'si ve Şerhi - (Makāsıd-ı Aliyye fî Şerhi't-Tâiyye)*, edited by Mehmed Demirci (Istanbul: Vefa yayınları 2007), 65–66.

into Ottoman Turkish a saying of one of the Sufi masters, the Shaykh continues his analysis:

> 'According to the Sufis, love is either a mystical state (*hâl*) or a spiritual station (*makâm*). As the scholastic doctors (*mütekellîmin*) have said: love (*muhabbet*) is the inclination of the heart and spirit toward something in which a perfect understanding is obtained. If the devotee realizes this reality, understanding this, he will apprehend that that perfect truth and understanding is nothing other than inclination for God Himself. That is why the devotee who sees naught else but the true perfection, sees Him by Him, by His Power and through Him. So the devotee's love of God is by virtue of His will and by means of His contemplation. And for this reason, such love demands obedience to the Beloved and this sort of eternal, divine love is ultimately expressed by following the path of obedience to God.[46]

In the third part of *The Pilgrims' Path,* Anqarawī describes the hundred steps which lead up to the divine unity, each of which is subdivided in turn into ten chapters with ten degrees. Chapter seven opens with two degrees: *muhabbet* and *'aşk*, the latter being presented as the superior form of love. Discussing *'aşk* in the second paragraph, he begins out by citing Ibn 'Arabī's statement that 'Passionate love (*'ishq*) is the inclination of love back on itself'.[47] Here, as in all of his works, Anqarawī often cites the words of Sufi masters to elucidate the topic. In an interesting passage he describes how 'perfect love (*kemâl-i aşk*) annihilates (*fânî kıla*) the lover (*âşık*) and destroys, after being enkindled with fiery longing for the beloved (*ma'şūk*), everything that is not eternal in him'.[48] In this degree, the lover seems to attain a more important inner spiritual state in which his love is purified and he is utterly preoccupied with Him. The Shaykh ends this paragraph with the following words:

---

46. İsmail Rusûhî Ankaravî, *Minhâcü'l-Fukarâ. Mevlevî Âdâb ve Erkânı Tasavvuf Istılahları*, edited by Sah Arpaguş (Istanbul: Vefa Yayınları, 2008), 402.
47. *'al-'ishq iltifāt al-ḥubb 'alā al-ḥubb'*, İsmail Rusûhî Ankaravî, *Minhâcü'l-Fukarâ. Mevlevî Âdâb ve Erkânı Tasavvuf Istılahları*, 406.
48. İsmail Rusûhî Ankaravî, *Minhâcü'l-Fukarâ. Mevlevî Âdâb ve Erkânı Tasavvuf Istılahları*, 406.

> The degree of love (*mertebe-i 'aşk*) superior to the [degree of] intelligence and to the flight of the imagination, for it strips the veil off [the countenance of] the Glorious Majesty.[49]

Therefore love (*'ishq*, or *'aşk* in Turkish) is something that a human being cannot really understand or comprehend within himself. In this sense, love is eternal and boundless.

Conclusion: Boundless Love

In the end we arrive back at our point of origin. The true lover is every human being who approaches the boundless love of God even if his love be but a romantic and figurative attachment, even if his aim be a human rather than divine object. Love, considered as a relationship between two human beings, as an inclination towards desiring someone else, is the basis of every kind of love, yet passionate love (*'ishq*) remains superior in degree, being ultimately the point of culmination of love since this higher inclination and intention is engraved in the heart of humanity. Such love, such *'ishq*, is boundless because it is the primordial character of the Divinity. From an Islamic Sufi perspective it could not be otherwise. Anqarawī's texts on the idea of love that we have translated and discussed above represent an attempt at a systematic understanding of the erotic theology of Muslim mysticism.

Muhabbet represents a general feeling of longing, or better said, man's primordial emotional force directed towards something or someone, as reflected in God Himself who is reflected in the world. Since the force of *muhabbet* in the human being has an innate tendency to aspire upwards towards God; when man's will is inspired by this love, he discovers a reflex of the boundless love of God (*muhabbet*) that is grounded in the unlimited Divine Will. While the powers of human comprehension must confined to a certain *ratio*, moderation and measure, love cannot be confined by nor forced to submit to this same law. That is the reason why the saints and the mystics act independent of any worldly rationale.

Considered chronologically, as a technical term in Muslim mysticism, we can say that *muhabbet* is the basic philosophical

49. İsmail Rusûhî Ankaravî, *Minhâcü'l-Fukarâ. Mevlevî Âdâb ve Erkânı Tasavvuf Istılahları*, 408.

concept of love in Islam. In this perspective, *muhabbet* also naturally expresses the basic attitude of Sufi love mysticism, alluding to the general movement of the human will, and in this sense is also superior to all other desires. That's why Anqarawī ends with speculation on the meaning of loving-kindness or *muhabbet* when commenting on the Rūmī's question, 'What is the lover?'. Anqarawī exploited the general concept of love to define the status of the person who is subject to the influence of the *'ishq*. To the question of who is the passionate lover, he responded that the lover is one who experiences *muhabbet*, general love, in his life. Anqarawī's aim here is to give a philosophical answer to the question, for which the more general term of *muhabbet* seems more appropriate.

Theoretically speaking, *'ishq* is superior to *muhabbet* because it penetrates more profoundly into the realm of *muhabbet* itself. In the metaphysical order, according to the Sufi thinkers, *'ishq* represents a kind of point of departure for love from its finite condition—it is the beginning of love's infinite boundlessness as it approaches closer to the Divinity. With respect to the general idea of *muhabbet*, it can be said that *'ishq* amplifies the unlimited will to unite with the object of love. In other words, *'ishq* itself demands union with the Beloved. That is why the word in some Islamic languages influenced by Arabic primarily denotes human erotic passion: the sensual love between man and woman.[50]

'Ishq is powerful because it is without limits, just as God's love is infinite and limitless. It is quite comprehensible how the concept of *'ishq* in its boundlessness could be intimately associated with God's boundless love. Rābi'a, among the first mystics—let us emphasise, a woman—to use the word *'ishq* in the lexicon of Muslim mysticism, used the term in respect to her own relationship of boundless and infinite love for the divinity. The love for God, she understood, must be free from any kind of fear, especially fear of Hell and its punishments, and from any kind of regard for the pleasures coming from hope for paradise. This is one sense of the boundlessness of love. Her discourse concerns a love that loves God without regard for anything else. Such love which is boundless without desiring anything extraneous to God typifies the powerful feeling of love that is the reality of *'ishq*.

---

50. Leonard Lewisohn, 'Romantic Love in Islam', in *Encyclopædia of Love in World Religions*, edited by Yudit Greenberg (New York: Macmillan Reference & Thomson Gale 2007), volume II, 513–15

In this perspective, both *muhabbet* and *'ishq* are probably in the same situation of boundlessness, although if *'ishq* is superior to *muhabbet*, it must be even more boundless.

To sum up, we can say that any kind of love which reflects God's love is potentially boundless. That is exactly what Elif Shafak tries to depict in her novel about Rūmī and Shams' relationship. Reading this novel—as superficially romantic as can appear in some ways—one notices that the human feelings of love in all the various social situations and romantic circumstances discussed therein are really quite profound and deep expressions of love because they are all related to the Divinity. *The Forty Rules of Love* all stem from God and flow through human beings, who are creatures of a divine origin. Finally, Shafak's novel gives a remarkable overview of these varieties of love (*muhabbet, 'ishq*), illustrating both Rūmī's notion of his love of God, for human beings and for all creatures as he approaches the boundless Divinity.

The question of superiority of *'ishq* over *muhabbet* stands at a critical point. In the preface of the Second Book, Anqarawī seems to return to the idea of *muhabbet* for explaining the status of lover. It would seem that he needed this concept to describe love and, in this way, the term *muhabbet* takes priority in his treatise. But is *muhabbet* really inferior to *'ishq*? A famous couplet of Rūmī can help us to find a solution. The mystic affirms: 'Whether Eros hails from hither or Yonder, it will lead us ultimately back Yonder.'[51] The verse implies that the goal of every 'love' is the Beloved, God Himself and for this reason virtually all types of love may potentially lead to the same divine source, since they originate in the summons from Him Who is beyond human understanding. In *The Pilgrims' Path* Anqarawī reached a similar conclusion regarding *'ishq*, penning this quatrain that excellently encapsulates the idea of love's boundlessness:

> Love (*'ishq*) is superior to comprehension,
> to the attributes of separation or union.
> Whatever appears beyond the imagination
> Shades our understanding and reflection.[52]

---

51. *Mathnawī*, I: 111.
52. İsmail Rusûhî Ankaravî, *Minhâcü'l-Fukarâ. Mevlevî Âdâb ve Erkânı Tasavvuf Istılahları*, 408.

Bibliography

Abou-Bakr, Omaima. 'Abrogation of the Mind in the Poetry of Jalal al-Din Rumi', in *Alif: Journal of Comparative Poetics*, 14 (1994): 37-63.

Ambrosio, Alberto Fabio. *Dervisci. Storia, antropologia, mistica*, Rome: Carocci editore, 2011.

_______. 'Ismā'īl Rusūhī Anqarawī: An Early Mevlevi Intervention into the Emerging Kadızadeli-Sufi Conflict', *Sufism and Society: Arrangements of the Mystical in the Muslim World, 1200–1800*, edited by J Curry and E Ohlander, London & New York: Routledge, 2011, pp. 183-197.

_______. *Vie d'un derviche tourneur: Doctrine et rituels du soufisme au XVIIe siècle*, Paris: CNRS Editions, 2010.

_______. 'Galata Mevlevihanesi'nde Şeyh Olmak/Being a Shaykh in Galata', in *Saltanatın Dervişleri Dervişlerin Saltanatı İstanbul'da Mevlevilik = The Dervishes of Sovereignty, The Sovereignty of Dervishes: The Mevlevi Order in Istanbul.* Istanbul: Istanbul Araştırmalar Enstitüsü, 2007, 42–56.

_______. 'Ecrire et décrire la confrérie Mevlevîyye entre le XVIe et XVIIe siècle', R Chih, C Mayeur-Jaouen, D Gril, R McGregor (editors), Le soufisme à l'époque ottomane, Institut Français d'archéologie orientale IFAO, Le Caire, 2010, 275–290.

Ambrosio, AF, E Pierunek, and Th Zarcone, *Les derviches tourneurs: Doctrine, histoire et pratiques*, Paris: Les Editions du Cerf, 2006.

Ankarawî, İsmail Rüsûhî. *Mecmûatü'l-Letâif ve Metmûratü'l Maarif (Şerhü'l-Mesnevî)*. 7 volumes Istanbul: Matbaa-i Âmire, 1289/1872.

_______. *Sharḥ-i kabīr-i Anqarawī bar Mathnawī-yi Mawlawī*, translated into Persian by 'Iṣmat Sattārzādah: 15 volsume, Tehran: Zarrın 1374 A.Hsh./1995; reprinted several times.

_______. *Minhâcü'l-Fukarâ. Mevlevî Âdâb ve Erkânı Tasavvuf Istılahları*, edited by Safi Arpaguş, Istanbul: Vefa Yayınları, 2008.

_______. *Osmanlı Tasavvuf Düşüncesi: İbn'ül-Fârız'ın Kasîde-i Tâiyye'si ve Şerhi - (Makāsıd-ı Aliyye fî Şerhi't-Tâiyye)*, edited by Mehmed Demirci, Istanbul: Vefa Yayınları, 2007.

Anvar-Chenderoff, Leili. *Rūmī*, Paris: Editions Entrelacs, 2004.

Aquinas, Thomas. *The Summa Theologica of St Thomas Aquinas*, Second revised edition, 1920, translated by Fathers of the English Dominican Province, Online Edition, 2008.

Arı, Ahmet. *Galib Dede'nin aşk ateşi Şeyh Galib Divanı'nda aşk*, Istanbul: Profil Yayıncılık, 2008.

Badawī, 'Abd al-Rahman. *Shahīdat al-'Ishik al-ilâhī, Râbi'a al-Adawīyya*, third edition, Cairo, 1976.

Baldick, Julian. 'The Legend of Rābi'a of Baṣra: Christian Antecedents, Muslim Counterparts', in *Religion*, 20 (1990): 233–47.

Binyamin, Abrahamov. *Divine Love in Islamic Mysticism. The Teaching of al-Ghazālī and al-Dabbāgh*, London & New York: RoutledgeCurzon, 2003.

Ceyhan, Semih. *İsmail Ankaravî ve Mesnevî Şerhi*, Phd Thesis, Bursa: T. C. Uludağ Üniversitesi Sosyal Bilimler Enstitüsü Temel İslam Bilimleri Anabilim Dalı Tasavvuf Bilim Dali, 2005.

Çam, Nusret. *Aşk dini*, Istanbul: Ötüken Neşriyat, 2010.

Çetindağ, Yusuf. *Aşk üzerine*, Istanbul: Kitabevi, 2011.

Chittick, William. *The Sufi Path of Love: The Spiritual Teachings of Rumi*, Albany: State University of New York Press, 1983.

Dakake, Maria. 'Guest of the Inmost Heart: Conceptions of the Divine Beloved among Early Sufi Women', in *Comparative Islamic Studies*, 3 (2007): 72–97.

al-Daylami, Ali b. Muhammad. *A Treatise on Mystical Love: Abū'l-Ḥasan 'Alī b. Muḥammad al-Daylamī*, translated by JN Bell & HM Abdul Latif Al Shafie, Edinburgh: Edinburgh University Press, 2005.

al-Ghazālī, Abū Ḥāmid. *L'Amore di Dio*. Italian translation by Carla Fabrizi, Bologna: EMI, 2004.

Gölpınarlı, Abdülbâki. *Mevlânâ'dan sonra Mevlevilik*, Istanbul: İnkılâp ve Aka, 1982.

Ibn 'Arabi. *al-Futuhat al-Makkiyya*, 4 volumes, Cairo, 1911.

Ibn al-Fāriḍ, 'Umar. *'Umar Ibn al-Fāriḍ: Sufi Verse, Saintly Life*, translated by Emil Homerin, New York/Mahwah NJ: Paulist Press, 2001.

Jan van Gelder, Geert. 'Rābi'a's Poem on the Two Kinds of Love: A mystification?' in *Verse and the Fair Sex. Studies in Arabic Poetry and in Representation of Women in Arabic Literature.* A Collection of papers presented at the 15th Congress of the Union Européenne des Arabisants et Islamisants (Utrecht/Driebergen, September 13-19, 1990), Frederich de Jong, editor, Utrecht: Publications of the MT Houtsma Strichting, 1993, 66–76.

Lewis, Franklin D. *Rumi. Past and Present, East and West: the Life, Teaching and Poetry of Jalâl al-Din Rumi*, Oxford: Oneworld Publications, 2000.

Rūmī, Jalāl al-Dīn. *The Masnavi. Book Two*, translated with an Introduction and Notes by Jawid Mojaddedi, Oxford: Oxford University Press, 2007.

_______. Reynold A Nicholson (editor) *Mathnawī-yi maʿnawī*, edited RA Nicholson. Tehran: Dībā, 1378 A.Hsh./1999.

_______. *The Mathnawí of Jalálu'ddín Rúmí*, edited and translated RA Nicholson, EJ W Gibb Memorial. London: Luzac & Co, 1925–1937, 8 volumes.

Safavi G. and Simon Weightman. *Rūmī's Mystical Design: Reading the* Mathnawī, *Book One*, Albany: SUNY Press, 2009.

Safi, Omid. 'Did the Two Oceans Meet? Connections and Disconnections between Ibn al-ʿArabī and Rūmī', in *Journal of the Muhyiddin Ibn ʿArabi Society*, XXVI (1999): 55–88.

Scattolin, Giuseppe (ed.). *Poems of Ibn al-Farid, The Dīwān of Ibn al-Fāriḍ. Readings of its Text Throughout History*, Cairo: Institut Français d'Archéologie Orientale, 2004.

Shafak, Elif. *The Forty Rules of Love: A novel of Rumi*, New York: Viking Penguin, 2010.

_______. = Şafak, Elif. *Aşk*, Istanbul: Doğan Yayıncılık, 2009.

Silvers, Laury. '"God Loves Me:" The Theological Content and Context of Early Pious and Sufi Women's Sayings on Love', in *Journal of Islamic Studies*, 30 (2010): 33–59.

Smith, Margaret. *Rabiʿa. The Life & Work of Rabiʿa and Other Women Mystics in Islam*, Oxford: Oneworld, 1994.

Yağmurn Sinan. *Aşkın gözyaşları Şems-i Tebrizi: biyografik roman*, Konya: Karatay Akademik Yayınları, 2010.

Yakıt, İsmail. *Mevlana'da aşk felsefesi*, Istanbul: Ötüken Neşriyat, 2010.

Yardım, Ali. *Mesnevî Hâdisleri (Tesbît ve Tahrîc)*, Istanbul: Damla Yayınevi, 2008.

Yasa, Metin. *Rubaileri ışığında Mevlana'da aşk ve işlevi*, Ankara: Elis Yayınları, 2010.

Zilfi, Madeline C. *The Politics of Piety: The Ottoman Ulema in the Postclassical Age (1600–1800)*, Minneapolis: Bibliotheca Islamica, 1988.